*Confederate Morale
and Church Propaganda*

JAMES W. SILVER received his education at the University of North Carolina, Peabody College, and Vanderbilt University, and taught for many years at the University of Mississippi, where he was chairman of the department of history from 1946 to 1957. In addition to *Confederate Morale and Church Propaganda,* he is the author of *Edmund Pendleton Gaines: Frontier General* (1949); *A Life for the Confederacy* (1959); *A Surgeon's Recollections* (1960); *Mississippi in the Confederacy* (1961); and *Mississippi: The Closed Society* (1964), as well as numerous articles in scholarly publications. He is professor of history at the University of Notre Dame.

Confederate Morale and Church Propaganda

By
JAMES W. SILVER

The Norton Library
W · W · NORTON & COMPANY · INC ·
NEW YORK

Books That Live
The Norton imprint on a book means that in the publisher's
estimation it is a book not for a single season but for the years.
W. W. Norton & Company, Inc.

PRINTED IN THE UNITED STATES OF AMERICA

1 2 3 4 5 6 7 8 9 0

Contents

	Preface	7
I.	The Clergy Leads the Way	13
II.	His Chosen People	25
III.	The Church Will Sound the Trumpets	42
IV.	For God and Country	64
V.	The Threat of Yankeeism	82
VI.	Not Even Bayonets Have Done More	93
	Bibliography	103
	Index	115

Preface

THE MAJOR CONCLUSION of the writer of this volume
is that anyone who has the temerity to venture into the
fields of both public opinion and religion in the nineteenth
century has the right to have his head examined. It all
started innocently enough. Some twenty-five years ago he
discovered, on reading books by Ella Lonn, Frank L. Owsley,
and Albert B. Moore, that the Confederacy had never existed
as the story books portrayed it. The legend of a united
people who went down fighting as one man against overwhelming odds simply could not stand serious investigation.
In reality the Confederacy had collapsed from within. Its
people had been divided from the start and as the "short"
summer war lengthened into weary years of fighting,
Southerners lost their will to fight. Real unity in the South
came only after Appomattox and after Reconstruction, too,
when those who were waging a desperate struggle against
poverty and disease and hopelessness paused long enough
to glance back at the "good old days." Newer generations
came along, more steeped in the traditions of the Lost Cause
than their ancestors had been energetic in defending it.

This is not to imply an interest in debunking the Confederacy or the Old South. There is glory enough in both
as they really were. But it has seemed logical to a recent
generation of Southern historians that, instead of defending
what has been, their job should be to explain why a state
such as Mississippi has had to wait a hundred years to
regain a prosperity she had in the 1850's. One doesn't have
to question the motivation of secessionist fire-eaters or to
debate whether they were right in principle in pointing out
the obvious fact that results have proved their judgment

tragically inept. At least three generations of Southerners have paid a terrible price for the erratic behavior of their Confederate ancestors. That's a fact.

In view of the heated agitations of this day it might be well for Southerners to ponder the course of action of their section a century ago. At least, it should be possible to avoid some of the same mistakes, although the present writer is not bold enough to point them out to those who will not see. He would suggest, though, that a great many people who voted even indirectly for secession in 1860 and 1861 did so on the basis of certain premises later to be found false. Secession would be peaceful, the South would get out of the Union in order to bargain effectively for its return, the British would intervene, the North would not fight, and if perchance she did, Yankee soldiers would never stand up to chivalrous Southrons in battle. So many leading citizens offered to drink all of the spilled blood that perhaps they might have done it, if they had not been otherwise occupied. These things, believed by many if not by all Southerners, certainly indicate that thirty years of emotional agitation had developed in the South by 1860 an orthodox and perhaps a closed mind. Result: the most colossal blunder in American history.

This essay is an attempt to show what part religion played in bringing on secession and in promoting the War Between the States. It is most emphatically not a history of the church. The author has no interest in religion as such, but sees the church solely as a powerful social organization. He still remembers his shock at the realization that Confederate society contained the seeds of its own destruction. He has since been collecting for almost twenty years various kinds of evidence which might show how and why civilian morale in the Confederacy deteriorated as it did. His primary interest has been in the various forces which helped to sustain and elevate the morale of a hard-pressed people. There is not the slightest doubt in his mind that the most powerful agency of this nature was the church.

Here the record speaks pretty much for itself. Because of the controversial nature of the subject, the writer has used many—perhaps too many—quotations. These have not been taken out of context and there have been few conclusions drawn, moral or otherwise. His illustrations have been taken from voluminous notes, many of which could have been discarded and others substituted without changing the picture.

It was customary in ante-bellum days for Southerners to defend slavery as a system superior to that of so-called free labor in the North. Today one of the usual defenses of the "Southern way of life" is an attack on social conditions in the North. In like fashion, if one is interested in blame and censure, a case can easily be made that Northern churches had taken an aggressive attitude toward slavery, that they were in considerable degree responsible for the war, and that they used the same tactics as did their counterparts in the South. But so far as the volume at hand is concerned, this is all beside the point—the present study has to do neither with blame nor praise, and it deals with the South only.

An excursion into the fascinating possibilities of the influence of public opinion on the conduct of churchmen tempted but dismayed the author. He would have preferred, also, to have studied more carefully the effect of church propaganda on the slave and free Negro population of the South, but his evidence did not seem to warrant it.

There is unquestionably much room for error in a subjective study of this sort. It seems reasonable, for instance, that the more extreme and emotional high priests were the ones who got their views into print. The agitators, whether newspaper editors, politicians, or preachers, were the ones heard most loudly. Even-tempered, moderate people went about their work quietly, without an eye to the headlines. Thus, the documents now available for study may present a one-sided picture of the times. Unfortunately, there were no public opinion polls in those days, although every Confederate who could write seems to have kept a diary. Whether the writer has been able to assemble an accurate story of the use of the church as an instrument of propaganda is for the reader to judge.

The material for this monograph has been taken from extensive notes, collected over a period of two decades, on the larger question of public opinion in the Confederacy. In view of the detailed references in the text, it would be superfluous to list all sources used, though it may be said that the study is based broadly on sermons, church newspapers, and the minutes of denominational organizations. For those hardy souls who would further pursue the matter or who wish to check on original documents, there is now available a magnificent two-volume guide, compiled by Marjorie Lyle Crandall, *Confederate Imprints: A Check List Based Principally on the Collection of the Boston Athenaeum* (Boston, 1955).

In the course of his study the author has visited the following college and university libraries: Emory University, University of Florida, University of Georgia, Harvard University, University of Mississippi, Mississippi College, University of North Carolina, University of Richmond, University of Texas, and Tulane University; private libraries: Boston Athenaeum, Confederate Library and Museum, Henry E. Huntington Library, and Union Theological Seminary; state libraries and archives in Atlanta, Austin, Jackson, Montgomery, Nashville, Raleigh and Richmond; state historical society libraries in Nashville and Richmond; and Federal libraries and archives in Washington.

For travel and study the author has been the grateful recipient of grants allocated by the Social Science Research Council, the University of Mississippi, and the Huntington Library. He was also able to spend a great many profitable hours in the magnificent Confederate collection in the Boston Athenaeum while a Ford fellow at Harvard University.

University of Mississippi   James W. Silver
Fall, 1956

Confederate Morale
and Church Propaganda

CHAPTER I

The Clergy Leads the Way

In the hot summer of 1862 a Texan volunteer serenely observed that Richmond has been saved by providential intervention. "It seems to me," he wrote, "that [McClellan] trusted in his powerful army for success. He had the best drilled men, the best arms the ingenuity of man could invent . . . drilled cannons & . . . even steel breastplates. Just think of his weak & feeble thrust in comparison to God's powerful arm of assistance. So I pray to God for success. I thank God for health and look to him for strength—turn me from God and I am a miserable wreck."[1]

Albert H. Clark, a young Mississippian about to leave Oxford with a newly raised company, felt the same way: "Well, Bill, we can never be conquered only by the ruling power of God but alas! if God is against us, we are ruined forever."[2] Another soldier assured his "Precious Wife" that "when we lay *all* upon the altar of our country, The God of Nations will give us a permanent happy existence. How near akin is patriotism to religion."[3] Lewis Burwell, ready to enter the 1864 Virginia campaign, was certain "that to die I shall but leave a world of Sin for my eternal home of bliss."[4] And in Charleston, Tennessee, a Richmond College volunteer on his deathbed requested his family not to grieve,

[1] Letters of William C. Chambers, S. M. Wood, J. A. Morris and J. H. Chambers, 1862 (typescript in University of Texas Library, Austin), p. 42.
[2] Clark to William H. McDonald, n.d. (in possession of Mrs. Calvin Brown, Oxford, Miss.).
[3] Soldier to "Precious Wife," Feb. 19, 1862 (in Brock Collection, Henry E. Huntington Library, San Marino, Cal.).
[4] Burwell to H. W. Rison, April 27, 1864 (in *ibid.*).

for "It will only be a little while until we meet in Heaven. I go to the Mansion not made with hands. Tell my pastor that death has no shadow of a fear for me. I felt I was going straight home."[5]

Such professions of unquestioning belief can be duplicated a thousand times in intimate Confederate letters. They reveal a simple faith of "a people who acknowledge the hand of God in every event,"[6] a faith based on the assurance of personal salvation and divine interposition in everyday affairs, buttressed by a literal reading of the Scriptures. A tiny un-paged tract entitled "Bethel," designed to bolster the fighting man's morale, proudly boasted of the lack of infidels in the South: "The atheistic and fanatical heresies, that have so sadly corrupted Northern society, and have weakened the power of scriptural faith and piety, have not seriously demoralized Southern society."[7] Few were likely to scoff at the notion that Lieutenant Mangum of the Sixth North Carolina Regiment had been divinely preserved when at Manassas a bullet struck the Bible in his pocket. The Lieutenant died anyway, but not until, according to God's plan, he had grasped the opportunity to "look to the Mercy Seat."[8]

A people in whose lives religion played such an integral part could easily and perhaps somewhat eagerly believe in the miraculous escape from casualties of the Oglethorpe Rifles who went into the thick of battle at the precise moment the homefolk were praying for their safety.[9] Charleston, Richmond, Petersburg, and Macon were "pre-

[5] William H. McIntosh, *James C. Sumner, The Young Soldier Ready for Death* (Marion, Ala., 1862), p. 5.

[6] Proclamation of Governor William H. Gist, as quoted in Thomas Smyth, *The Sin and the Curse; or The Union, The True Source of Disunion, and Our Duty in the Present Crisis* (Charleston, 1860), p. 3.

[7] Copy in Curry Pamphlets (Alabama State Department of Archives and History, Montgomery), vol. XXXIV.

[8] Adolphus W. Mangum, *Myrtle Leaves; or Tokens at the Tomb* (Raleigh, 1864), pp. 29-32.

[9] E. Merton Coulter, *The Confederate States of America, 1861-1865* (Baton Rouge, 1950), pp. 529-530.

served in answer to prayer"[10] and a Yankee raid on the principal salt works of the Confederacy was repulsed because made on Sunday[11]—the same *post-mortem* suggested by New York preachers to explain the Northern debacle at First Manassas.[12] Late in the war Sherman's troops came within eight miles of Chester, South Carolina, "but an All Wise Providence protected us" and turned them off on a different road to Lancaster.[13] What the Lancastrians thought of this change in plans is not a matter of record.

There was little surprise, then, in the prophecy of the *Southern Episcopalian,* happy over the acknowledgment of God in the Confederate Constitution, that "a sense of religion will animate our people and sustain them under any difficulties with which they may have to contend . . . we shall need the consolation of divine comfort, and the sense of divine support."[14] The editor was right on both counts.

This dependence on religion in the Confederacy may be one more reason for associating the Civil War with the age of chivalry. It made possible the use of the church as the most effective means of arousing and sustaining the morale of a people hardly conscious of the pressing need for an all-out effort. Instruments for carrying out this mission were readily at hand in the lay and clerical leadership, the individual churches with their organization into synods, conferences, and associations, and the religious press.

Academicians have long and fruitlessly argued whether the politicians led the people or were themselves dragged into secession. It may have been in the nature of a photo-finish. In any case the broad basis of preparation had been laid by a generation's crusade which had convinced Southerners of the divinity of the institution of slavery and of

[10] Richmond (Va.) *Sentinel,* Oct. 19, 1861; Frank E. Vandiver (ed.), *The Civil War Diary of General Josiah Gorgas* (University, Ala., 1947), p. 51.
[11] Richmond (Va.) *Christian Observer and Presbyterian Witness,* Dec. 1, 1864 (hereinafter cited as *Christian Observer*).
[12] Thomasville (Ga.) *Southern Enterprise,* Aug. 28, 1861.
[13] C. L. Robertson to Wesson, March 13, 1865 (in Brock Collection).
[14] VII, 656 (March, 1861).

their holy duty to protect it. Even so, until Lincoln's call
for troops, a majority of the slave states held to the Union
and those seven which had pulled out within three months
of the election of the first Republican president did so on
the basis of reasoning soon to prove illusory.[15] Clear judgment was unlikely in a region where orthodox thinking had
become the rage and an emotion-packed passion for unanimity had taken hold of the people.

Secession in the church was a natural prelude to secession
in the state. In 1850, when Calhoun noted in his last formal
speech that the bonds of unity between North and South
were beginning to snap, he undoubtedly had in mind the
spiritual cords that had bound together the Methodists and
Baptists. Although formal separation in most churches
came only after war had begun, it has been surmised that
intra-denominational squabbles were not only a major signal
of disunion sentiment, but were also "the chief cause of the
final break."[16] When Northern humanitarians accelerated
their agitation against slavery, the South responded by
proscribing Yankee teachers, texts, and propaganda in the
form of Beecher's sermons, Whittier's poems, and Sumner's
discourses.[17]

Religious fire-eaters, such as the intellectual "Calhoun of
the Church," James H. Thornwell, and his younger protegé,
Benjamin M. Palmer, have long been allocated their rightful
places with Robert Barnwell Rhett and William Lowndes
Yancey. The learned Thornwell, easily the pre-eminent
Presbytyerian in South Carolina, in a fast-day discourse a
fortnight after Lincoln's election, called for secession, even
though "our path to victory may be through a baptism of
blood."[18] After the break of South Carolina, writing "to
influence public opinion in states which have not seceded,"

---

[15] See above, Preface, pp. 8-9.
[16] William W. Sweet, *The Story of Religions in America* (New York,
1930), pp. 448-449.
[17] George E. Naff, "Cleveland's Text Books," *Quarterly Review of
the Methodist Episcopal Church, South*, XV, 63-75 (Jan., 1861) ; Nashville (Tenn.) *Christian Advocate*, Jan. 19, 1860.
[18] "Our National Sins; Preached in First Presbyterian Church, Columbia, S. C., November 21, 1860," in *Fast Day Sermons, or, The
Pulpit on the State of the Nation* (New York, 1861), pp. 55-56.

he declared, "A free people can never consent to their own degradation" in becoming a subject province or submitting to political annihilation. But he held out the prospect of a division of the country into two great nations "without a jostle or a jar."[19]

Nevertheless, it was "the big villain of the play," the eloquent Palmer, who catapulted himself into the limelight as the secessionist orator of the day with his Thanksgiving sermon in New Orleans. Feeling "impelled to deepen the sentiment of resistance in the southern mind," Palmer struck fire with God's plan for the South—to perpetuate slavery—and the sublimity of the Southern position: "If she has the grace given her to know her hour she will save herself, the country, and the world."[20] Printed in the *Daily Delta* for the third time early in December, 1860, this throwback to Thomas Paine was broadcast in some fifty thousand pamphlets which gathered a fearful harvest.

Thornwell and Palmer were merely the spectacular leaders of thousands of preachers, editors, and church officials who by their very calling were in a position to impress most deeply a highly religious people. Thomas W. Caskey, minister of the Christian church in Jackson, set out with the Attorney General of Mississippi "to talk the people out of the Union."[21] Bishop Francis H. Rutledge promised to pay into the Florida treasury five hundred dollars when the state seceded.[22] Catholic Bishop Augustine Verot of Savannah blamed the Northern Protestant clergy with bringing on "this deplorable state of things," and rejoiced in secession.[23] The Reverend Thomas Smyth of Charleston scored the North for having perverted the Bible and God's

---

[19] *The State of the Country* . . . (Columbia, 1861), p. 13.

[20] "Thanksgiving Day Discourse; Delivered in the First Presbyterian Church, New Orleans, November 29, 1860," reprinted in *DeBow's Review*, XXX, 324-336 (Feb., 1861).

[21] John K. Bettersworth, *Confederate Mississippi* (Baton Rouge, 1943), p. 285.

[22] *Journal of the Proceedings of the Convention of the People of Florida* . . . (Tallahassee, 1861), p. 20.

[23] Benjamin J. Blied, *Catholics and the Civil War* (Milwaukee, 1945), pp. 63-64.

truth,[24] while in the same state Benjamin Franklin Perry became so incensed with the preachers' zeal in plunging the country into war that he stopped attending church.[25] Methodist pastors returning home by train from the Georgia Conference at Augusta favored secession by a vote of eighty-seven to nine.[26] On November 17, 1860 the Reverend James C. Wilson addressed his congregation in Gonzales, Texas:

It may be that if you behave yourselves very circumspectly and give them no cause to be angry with you, lie still where they have thrown you—though they now have the power to overwhelm you . . . with destructive laws, hot as the hellish passions of their own black hearts, foul as streams from the sewers of Pandemonium—they will not be cruel, they will defer your utter destruction yet a little longer, . . . upon good behavior. If you will cringe and fawn and smile, perhaps they will not kick you. . . . I think that perhaps the philosopher who first made the discovery of Southern effeminacy viewed the world through glasses of Northern manufacture.[27]

The record is full of similar manifestations by official church bodies and by the religious press. A few days before the election of convention delegates in South Carolina, the Presbyterian Synod solemnly called on them to imitate their Revolutionary fathers and to stand up for their rights.[28] North Carolina Presbyterians, professing to speak for four-fifths of the Southern clergy and church members, called on all the slave states to make common cause "in this hour of extremity."[29] The Alabama, Mississippi, and South Carolina Baptists officially considered it the duty of their states

[24] *Op. cit.*, pp. 8-12.
[25] Lillian A. Kibler, *Benjamin Franklin Perry: South Carolina Unionist* (Durham, 1946), p. 362.
[26] Petersburg (Va.) *Daily Express*, Dec. 15, 1860.
[27] Untitled printed pamphlet (n.p., n.d., in University of Texas Library), pp. 2-3.
[28] Charles E. Cauthen, *South Carolina Goes to War, 1860-1865* (Chapel Hill, 1950), p. 44.
[29] *North Carolina Presbyterian* (April, 1861), quoted in R. L. Stanton, *The Church and the Rebellion: A Consideration of the Rebellion against the Government of the United States; and the Agency of the Church, North and South, in Relation thereto* (New York, 1864), p. 187.

to secede immediately.[30]   Although the editor of the Nashville *Christian Advocate* remained calm until the middle of
November, he was soon taking to task a warlike Unionist of
St. Louis: "Very well, Brother Kingsley.   When you have
gotten into your regimentals, loaded your musket, and fixed
the bayonet on, and are ready to subjugate the South, *please
pass by this way.*"[31]   As a reporter noticed, the farther one
moved into the lower South the denser became the secession
atmosphere.[32]   But even Richmond papers, such as the
Central Presbyterian, the *Religious Herald*, and the *Christian Observer and Presbyterian Witness*, were determined
that honor and self respect demanded a firm stand.[33]   In
prophetic tones a week before the meeting of South Carolina's convention, the *Southern Presbyterian* declared that
the very highest wisdom of the state, including judges
and ministers of the Gospel, had determined that the
Palmetto State "in the face of all obloquy, and ridicule,
and menaces, of all the wrath and contempt of those who
alternately curse and jeer her [was determined] to assert
her independence."[34]

This is not to imply that Southern churchmen unanimously supported secession, state rights, or the war.   Beset with
the reprehensible infirmity of forming a minority section
in a country ruled by the majority, the South had long
preached the doctrine of unified opinion but had never
reached that happy state of mind.   Although most of them
departed of their own free will or through persuasion,
well-known unionist divines remained even in the Gulf
States for the life of the Confederacy.   James A. Lyon,
pastor of the First Presbyterian Church in Columbus, Mississippi, opposed secession, criticized Davis, condemned the
war as the work of demagogues, and favored Reconstruc-

[30] Memphis (Tenn.) *Daily Appeal*, Dec. 9, 1860; Jesse L. Boyd, *A
Popular History of the Baptists in Mississippi* (Jackson, 1930), p. 109.
[31] Jan. 17, 1861.
[32] *Ibid.*, Dec. 20, 1860.
[33] Richmond (Va.) *Central Presbyterian*, Jan. 6, 1861; *Christian
Observer*, Jan. 31, Feb. 7, 21, 1861; Richmond (Va.) *Religious Herald*,
Jan. 10, Feb. 26, March 3, 1861.
[34] Columbia (S. C.), Dec. 15, 1860.

tion. Somehow, he held the esteem of his parishioners and in 1863 was selected as moderator of the Southern Presbyterian General Assembly.

Some churchmen of similar stripe did not fare so well in Mississippi. The Presbyterian evangelist, John H. Aughey, claimed that he had been insulted, imprisoned, starved, and would have been hanged if he had not escaped.[35] Others of that staunch breed fled to the North, though one, the Reverend James Phelan of Macon, was murdered after slipping away to the country.[36] Texas vigilantes chased many a Northern Methodist out of the state and weeks before Lincoln's election hanged the Reverend Anthony Bewley in Fort Worth.[37] The classic example of irascibility among Southern unionist preachers was William G. Brownlow, who used both his pulpit and his Knoxville *Whig* to preserve the United States. Before his forced departure northward, the "Fighting Parson" lashed out against his fellow ministers as "destroying, God-defying, and hell-deserving TRAITORS to their country."[38] The Memphis *Daily Appeal* wryly observed that Brownlow was fortunate in not living in South Carolina or Mississippi.[39]

Border-state clergy were usually adamant on slavery and the rights of the sovereign state, but they were more concerned with moderate action than their brethren to the south. Robert L. Dabney felt that ministers should seem to have no politics—"there were plenty of politicians to make the fire burn hot enough, without my help to blow it."[40] Dr. Dabney was sure that Lincoln's election was no cause for secession, that South Carolina's "wanton breach of federal compacts" had "*worsted*" the common cause, "forfeited the

[35] Lewis G. Vander Velde, *The Presbyterian Churches and the Federal Union, 1861-1869* (Cambridge, 1932), p. 292.

[36] Bettersworth, *op. cit.*, p. 288.

[37] *Christian Advocate*, Nov. 1, 1860.

[38] William R. Cooper, "Parson Brownlow: A Study of Reconstruction in Tennessee," *Southwestern Bulletin*, XIX, 6-7 (Dec., 1931).

[39] Dec. 8, 1860.

[40] Dabney to Moses Hoge, Jan. 4, 1861, quoted in Peyton H. Hoge, *Moses Drury Hoge: Life and Letters* (Richmond, 1899), p. 139; *Christian Observer*, Jan. 17, 1861.

righteous strength of our position," but that her precipitate
step compelled "us to shield her from the chastisement she
most condignly deserves. We must 'go it blind' and stand
or fall with South Carolina."[41] He deplored, even after
Fort Sumter, the "infamy which would attach to the Christianity of America, if . . . it were found impotent to save
the land from fratricidal war."[42] In contrast to Palmer,
the Reverend A. H. Boyd preached from his Winchester,
Virginia, pulpit an 1860 Thanksgiving sermon on the
"Benefits We Enjoy as a Nation."[43] After the formation
of the Confederacy in Montgomery, Bishop Atkinson and
ten pastors of the Episcopal, Presbyterian, Baptist, Methodist, and Lutheran churches in Wilmington, North Carolina,
issued an address to the clergy and laity appealing to them
to do all in their power toward conciliation, and to avert the
horrors of civil war.[44] As late as President Davis's first
fast day, June 13, 1861, Bishop William Meade, ashamed
of the church's part in breaking up the Union, called for
honorable and friendly terms in peace overtures.[45] For the
first six months of 1861 the *Central Presbyterian,* in spite
of its pro-Southern position, was quite hopeful that the crisis
would pass.[46] It was the happy boast of Episcopalians that
their church had worked for peace and a united country.
Bishops Rutledge, Davis, and Gregg expressed great sadness
on leaving the Union,[47] but like Meade, James H. Otey (who
had condemned the secession of South Carolina as a crimi-

[41] Hoge, *op. cit.,* pp. 140-141.

[42] *Ibid.,* p. 139.

[43] *Christian Observer,* Nov. 28, 1860.

[44] *Ibid.,* Feb. 21, 1861.

[45] *Address on the Day of Fasting and Prayer* . . . (Richmond, 1861), pp. 6-7.

[46] This Richmond journal claimed that much of the existing trouble had grown out of gross misrepresentation on both sides. Many papers were said to have been "so fiendish" in the work that Satan might almost afford to take his ease. But, wrote the editor on Jan. 6, the Union has failed and the country presents an aspect of sadness.

[47] Joseph B. Cheshire, *The Church in the Confederate States: A History of the Protestant Episcopal Church in the Confederate States* (New York, 1912), pp. 10-11.

nal action),[48] and Atkinson, they turned from conciliators into enthusiastic Confederates.

In Maryland, Kentucky, and Missouri the churches were almost hopelessly divided, as indicated by a twelve to eleven border-state vote against a strong union statement by the Old School Presbyterians meeting in Columbus, Ohio in June, 1862.[49] Not that there was serious question of basic loyalty to the United States by this time.[50] Robert J. Breckinridge, for thirty years an advocate of gradual emancipation in Kentucky, but one who despised the abolitionists, had proved as powerful a figure for the Union as Palmer was for the Confederacy.[51] The founder of the *Danville Quarterly Review* had also made known his views in a strong Thanksgiving Day sermon and exerted such influence that R. L. Stanton declared he could have carried Kentucky into the Confederate States of America, if he had been so disposed.[52] On the other hand, Dr. Stuart Robinson, a defender of slavery, kept attacking the "Spread Eagle Charity, Piety and Oratory" of the North until his Louisville *True Presbyterian* was suppressed by the military and he was forced to flee to Canada.[53] Likewise, Thomas A. Hoyt of Louisville declared in a National Fast Day (January 4, 1861) sermon that Kentuckians must not allow South Carolina to be assailed, that the Southern states must be permitted to leave the Union peaceably. He too was forced to leave the city.[54]

As with those in military service, there was much soul-searching among the clergy as to loyalty and a considerable exchange of churchmen between the sections occurred in 1861. Dr. Leyburn of Philadelphia actually swapped pastorates with the Reverend M. B. Grier of Wilmington, North

[48] Otey to George Harris, Dec. 12, 1960, in James E. Walmsley (cont.), "Documents—The Change of Secession Sentiment in Virginia in 1861," *American Historical Review*, XXI, 98 (Oct., 1925).

[49] Vander Velde, *op. cit.*, p. 115.

[50] *Ibid.*, pp. 108-109.

[51] *Ibid.*, pp. 37-38, 143-146.

[52] *Op. cit.*, pp. 201-202.

[53] Vander Velde, *op. cit.*, pp. 173-174.

[54] Stanton, *op. cit.*, pp. 211-212.

Carolina. William J. Hoge left New York City to take the place of Reverend John E. Annan in Charlottesville.[55] Lindsay H. Blanton resigned from his Versailles pulpit because Kentucky decided to stay in the Union.[56] In the case of John H. Bocock, pastor of the Bridge Street Presbyterian in Georgetown, who had suggested after Lincoln's call for troops that yellow fever in the course of the summer "would be worth seventy thousand troops *to us*," removal south was involuntary—and later this Confederate enthusiast was superintending the manufacture of munitions of war.[57] Still another minister was expelled from his charge in Elizabethtown, New Jersey.[58] But the strangest situation of all confronted Dr. S. B. McPheeters of St. Louis, when he was suddenly called upon in the fall of 1862 to baptize an infant, apparently dressed in Rebel colors, with the name of Sterling Price. The incident led to a loyalty hearing at which McPheeters, exercising a sort of fifth amendment obstinacy, refused to testify. Supported by his congregation, he was nevertheless ordered by the military to leave Missouri.[59]

Thus the picture is not precise and clear. It is obvious that love of the Union was a strong passion with many churchmen even in the Deep South and that secession was undertaken with heavy hearts. In the slave border-states a course of moderation was usually urged until a final decision had to be made. But the fact remains that the overwhelming majority of Southern clergymen had for a generation given the church's blessing to the institution of slavery and its right to spread into the territories. There was not the slightest doubt in their minds about the evils of abolition nor the almost sacred rights of the state as a sovereign entity. Because of Southern piety, clergymen were leaders of tremendous influence in every community. When the show-down came, the more militant men of God were easily

[55] Vander Velde, *op. cit.*, p. 291.
[56] *Central Presbyterian*, Aug. 14, 1861.
[57] Stanton, *op. cit.*, p. 209.
[58] Vander Velde, *op. cit.*, p. 290.
[59] *Ibid.*, pp. 308-309.

in the vanguard of the secession movement. Above all else they had been instrumental in creating a state of mind definitely "Southern," one which made possible the disruption of the Union.

CHAPTER II

His Chosen People

IN THE MIDDLE of the nineteenth century it was generally conceded that the great influences in life were of a religious nature. The primary purpose of existence with most people was eternal salvation. Therefore, it was deemed essential that the individual should conduct his everyday affairs in harmony with the wishes of a just and stern God. Slavery had long been accepted as a part of God's plan and if Southerners as a whole could be convinced that the Confederacy and the war were also of divine inspiration, they might well build up an indestructable morale. Because of the limited industrial resources of the South, the success of the Confederacy depended on the degree of intestinal fortitude developed by the man in the street and on the farm. He needed to identify himself as a member of God's chosen people and his country as a fulfillment of the destiny of history.

All nations "at this late period must be born amid the storm of revolution, and must win their way to a place in history through the baptism of blood," claimed Bishop Stephen Elliott in the despondent early days of 1862. Corruption in the United States after the passing of the Revolutionary fathers, together with the triumph of the expedient, the popular, and the successful, had proven the illusion of democracy and equality. Cruelty of the unbridled multitude had brought Elliott around to thinking favorably of monarchy, aristocracy, and an established church.[1] "The world combined cannot deprive a nation of its destined place in history," wrote James W. Miles a year later. He saw a Divine Providence directing with steady and intelligent hand the Confederacy, "commissioned by God to contend for and illustrate great principles, intimately connected with the progress of humanity." The South could accept its destiny and become a glory among the nations or refuse and be made a warning example for ages to come. "It is impiety to despair . . . and in the hour of [our country's] success we will feel a more solemn sense of duty as instruments for accomplishing her divinely appointed mission."[2] According to the Reverend J. Jones of Rome, Georgia, this was a sacred war: "If the rescue of the holy sepulchre from the infidel Moslem, induced three millions of men to lay their bones in the East, shall we not willingly contend to snatch the word of God from the modern infidel?"[3] "Nature and nature's God has marked us out for two nations," shouted the Reverend Mr. Daniel I. Dreher.[4] Charleston's Thomas Smyth urged that by the peculiar providence of God, the South had been given "the high and holy keeping, above all other conservators, of the Bible."[5] As Bishop Thomas Atkinson saw the situation, ". . . it is God who rides in this storm, and will direct the whirlwind."[6] The *Commonwealth* added: ". . . we should go into this war,

---

[1] *"New Wine Not To Be Put in Old Bottles."* A Sermon Preached in Christ Church, Savannah . . . (Savannah, 1862), pp. 6, 7, 14. As early as President Buchanan's fast day on Jan. 4, 1861 S. J. P. Anderson of the Central Presbyterian Church, St. Louis, declared that "God is at work. He often punishes nations by letting them go mad, and in an hour of infatuation find food for years of bitter and unavailing repentance . . . it may be that the terrible but needed trial by fire . . . will re-unite us." He put part of the blame on the preachers. "I will not allow myself to ask how many of them have stolen fire from God's altars to kindle the flames of sectional strife" (*The Dangers and Duties of the Present Crisis*, St. Louis, 1861), pp. 3, 12.
[2] *God in History. A Discourse Delivered before the Graduating Class of the College of Charleston* . . . (Charleston, 1863), pp. 28-30.
[3] T. Conn Bryan, "The Churches in Georgia During the Civil War," *Georgia Historical Quarterly*, XXXIII, 285 (Dec. 1949).
[4] *A Sermon* . . . (Salisbury, 1861), p. 4.
[5] *Op. cit.*, p. 17.
[6] *Christian Duty in the Present Time of Trouble* . . . (Wilmington, 1861), p. 5.

feeling as did David, that he who does his duty to his country, is but doing part of his duty to his God. To fight is now . . . a religious duty."[7]

History had never recorded, Benjamin M. Palmer thought, a more sublime example of moral heroism than the secession of South Carolina. Relying on nothing "save the righteousness of her cause and the power of God, she took upon her shield and spear as desperate and as sacred a conflict as ever made a State immortal. . . . The Genius of history has already wreathed the garland with which her brow shall be decked."[8] To him the war was the holiest battle of all time, a fight for home, fireside, family, freedom, civilization, and religion.[9] In a sermon published by request of the New Orleans Confederate Guards, with his text from *Second Chronicles*, 6:34-35, the great orator declared, "Eleven tribes sought to go forth in peace from the house of political bondage, but the heart of our modern Pharaoh is hardened, that he will not let Israel go." Separation had surely been decreed by God: "We have vainly read the history of our fathers, if we failed to see that from the beginning two nations were in the American womb."[10] For when a nation becomes too strong for its virtue it is a rule of God's government that it must be divided or destroyed. The South was destined for freedom because no people who had a right to be free, and had resolved to be free, had ever been subjugated.[11] Founded on "immutable laws of God," the Confederacy was pre-eminently "the cause of God himself."[12]

---

[7] May 6, 1861.
[8] *A Vindication of Secession and the South* . . . (Columbia, 1861), p. 20.
[9] Margaret B. DesChamps, "Benjamin Morgan Palmer, Orator-Preacher of the Confederacy," *Southern Speech Journal*, XIX, 18 (Sept., 1953).
[10] *National Responsibility Before God* . . . (New Orleans, 1861), pp. 5, 27.
[11] Augusta (Ga.) *Daily Chronicle and Sentinel*, March 4, 1863.
[12] *Sermons of Bishop Pierce and Rev. B. M. Palmer* . . . *Before the General Assembly* . . . (Milledgeville, 1863), p. 9. In a pamphlet published in 1864 "Cincinnatus" contended that "A premature government, assuming to put itself into the van of civilization, is always a miscarriage. The womb of time has its fixed periods of gestation, and men cannot hurry them" (*Address of the Atlanta Register to the People of the Confederate States*, Atlanta, 1864).

The Presbyterian *True Witness* of New Orleans took a quick look at history early in the war and noticed that the attack in Baltimore on Massachusetts troops had been ordered by Providence for the anniversary of the battle of Lexington. "Thus the same day beheld the first blood of '76 and '61—fortunate omen of the result."[13] In Houston's Christ Church Bishop Gregg warned his listeners that the race was not always to the swift. But the Lord God Omnipotent "will be now and ever the shield and buckler of all those who are oppressed with wrong. . . ."[14] Bishop George F. Pierce agreed that God's blessing was on the good, and sooner or later His curse would be on the bad.[15] Dr. Read felt that God had never destroyed a nation in which there was an evangelical church.[16] Convinced that "history is a prolonged vindication of moral law," the Reverend Mr. Alfred M. Randolph was sure that an ungodly government (the United States) might seem to succeed for a time, but that God was only raising it to a conspicuous post "in order to render more widely instructive the mockery of its triumph and the story of its fall."[17] As the cornerstone of the Confederacy, slavery was defended throughout the war. For instance, in the summer of 1861 Catholic Bishop Augustus Martin of Natchitoches, Louisiana, described the institution as an eminently Christian one by which millions passed "from intellectual darkness to the sweet brilliance of the Gospel," and this in spite of the hypocritical sentimentality of Northern Puritans.[18].

In May, 1861 the Baptist Special Committee on the State of the Country concluded that Davis's administration was "contributing to the transcendent Kingdom of our Lord Jesus Christ,"[19] and the Y.M.C.A. of New Orleans asked

[13] April 27, 1861.

[14] *Journal of the 13th Annual Convention of the Protestant Episcopal Church in the Diocese of Texas* . . . (Houston, 1862), p. 32.

[15] *The Word of God A Nation's Life* . . . (Augusta, 1862), p. 14.

[16] *Christian Observer*, March 6, 1862.

[17] *Address on the Day of Fasting and Prayer* . . . (Fredericksburg, 1861), p. 9.

[18] Blied, *op. cit.*, p. 25.

[19] *Proceedings of the Southern Baptist Convention* . . . (Richmond, 1861), p. 63.

its Northern membership, "Has it not occurred to you, brethren, that the hand of God MAY BE in this political division, that both governments may effectually work out His designs in the regeneration of the World?"[20]

"Our cause is a just, nay, a holy one," cried Henry N. Pierce in Mobile on the Confederacy's first official fast day,[21] while J. C. Mitchell of the same city inquired, "Who can fail to see the hand of God in the whole movement?"[22] Christianity sanctioned the Confederacy, according to Edward T. Winkler: "As Christians, they might wear the plumed and brazen helm, and thrust the two-edged sword into the passionate heart of battle."[23] Before the Georgia legislature the Reverend Henry Tucker, professor of belles-lettres at Mercer University, maintained that "GOD is in the war. He brought it upon us." The Lord often used the wicked (in this case, the North) for divine ends: "Thus the guilt of those who wage this diabolical war on the un-offending people of these Confederate States, finds no apology in the providence of God."[24] In similar vein, Thomas V. Moore believed that war was simply an agency by which the Lord disciplines nations and that a long course of peace tends "to emasculate and corrupt a people," while war breaks up "mammon worship and effeminacy."[25]

The Presbyterian Synod of North Carolina sent word to its churches in November, 1861 that "We have no fear of the final issue. In His name we desire to set up our banners, feeling assured that it is a great moral and religious struggle, in which we are contending at once for the dearest rights of man, and for the purity, freedom and glory of the Church of God."[26] A few weeks later the Evangelical Lutheran Synod of South Carolina came to the same con-

---

[20] Quoted in Stanton, *op. cit.*, p. 181.
[21] *Sermon Preached in St. John's Church, Mobile* ... (Mobile, 1861), p. 6.
[22] *Fast Day Sermon* ... (Mobile, 1861), p. 30.
[23] *Duties of the Citizen Soldier* ... (Charleston, 1861), p. 7.
[24] *God in the War* ... (Milledgeville, 1861), pp. 7-9.
[25] *God Our Refuge and Strength in This War* ... (Richmond, 1861), p. 7.
[26] *Minutes of the Forty Eighth Sessions of the Synod of North Carolina* ... (Fayetteville, 1862), p. 23.

clusion, in recognizing "the hand of God in the wisdom of
Confederate councils and in the heroism of its defenders."[27]
United Presbyterians in Virginia felt that God held the
destiny of the Confederacy in the hollow of His hand,[28] and
the *Southern Lutheran* went along with the Reverend
Mathew Dance who declared, "I feel as if the Southern
Confederacy will be the Lord's peculiar people."[29]

Southern churchmen believed categorically that God intervened in the conduct of men so as to make them work out
His own purpose, and that, if the South went into the war
with the right spirit, "when the shock of invasion comes
the Lord will be here to repel it."[30]   In the April, 1863
Southern Presbyterian Review Thomas Smyth wrote of
"God's manifest presence and providence" with the Confederacy whose constitution was "sealed in the chancery
of Heaven."   God had entrusted the Southern people with
"an organized system of slave labor, for the benefit of the
world, and a blessing to themselves while imparting civil,
social, and religious blessings to their slaves. . . .   God
now spake as with a voice from heaven, saying 'Come out
of the Union, My People.'   Then came up from the millions
of hearts the shout, 'Go forward! for God is with us of a
truth.' "[31]   Thus Abraham Lincoln became another king of
Egypt and Jefferson Davis a second Moses. Such identifica-
tion of the cause of God with the cause of the Confederacy
is an indelible ingredient of Southern religious literature of
the war years.

[27] *Minutes of the Evangelical Lutheran Synod of South Carolina*
(Columbia, 1862), p. 24.
[28] *Proceedings of the Twenty-Second Annual Meeting of the Domestic
Missionary Society of Richmond* . . . (Richmond, 1861), p. 6.
[29] *Christian Observer*, Jan. 23, 1862.
[30] *Religious Herald*, June 13, 1861. ""It is a religious war," wrote
the editor of the *Christian Advocate*, May 9, 1861. "Is there any doubt
of the result of such a war?   Not in the world . . .   War and especially
a civil war imposes its religious duties, and it is a part of a religious
paper that is not a fossil . . .   to treat their duties in their season . . .
let us be careful to set the Lord always before us.   We do not answer
that the cause insures salvation, but we do unhesitatingly declare that
it is the cause to which divine providence has committed Christian
man . . .   and under God, Gideon's little band will triumph."
[31] Quoted in Stanton, *op. cit.*, p. 294.

Imbued with the notions that the war was necessary for purification and that righteousness of the cause decided every conflict, Southern churchmen developed an infallible formula. Every Confederate victory proved that God had shielded his chosen people and every defeat became the merited punishment of the same people for their sins. The war itself was a chastisement "inflicted by an Almighty arm."[32] "If the people . . . were to turn with one heart and one mind to the Lord . . . He would drive the invader from our territories. . . . He can turn them as He turns the rivers of water."[33] Put on an earthier basis, it was assumed, "That Providence which sustains the flight of a sparrow . . . might direct the death-bringing bullet to the vitals of our greatest chieftain."[34] Whenever rationalization for defeat seemed advisable, the preachers had only to glance about them to discover such sins as violation of the Sabbath, intemperance, demagoguery, corruption, luxury, impiety, murmuring, greed and avarice, lewdness, skepticism, "Epicurean expediency," private immorality, ill treatment of slaves, profanity, a proud and haughty spirit, speculation, bribery, boastfulness, and the "sin of all sins," covetousness.

A martial sermon preached in April, 1861 by J. H. Elliott declared that the Fort Sumter victory was the answer to prayer. Acknowledging the debt to Him who had "covered their heads in the day of battle," the minister confessed "the hand of God seems as plainly in it as in the conquest of the Midianites." Perhaps with an eye on the border states, he further suggested that "His Providence is fast uniting the whole South."[35] First Manassas brought forth a rash of messages which agreed with Stephen Elliott's sermon, delivered in Christ Church, Savannah, on a day of Thanksgiving called by Congress. The people had

[32] *Christian Observer*, May 9, 1861.

[33] J. W. Tucker, *God Sovereign and Man Free* (Fayetteville, 1862), p. 20.

[34] Tucker, *God in the War*, p. 12.

[35] *The Bloodless Victory. A Sermon Preached . . . on the Occasion of Taking Fort Sumter* (Charleston, 1861), p. 7.

humbled themselves on June 13 (Davis's first fast day) and the victory came as

the crowning token of his love—the most wonderful of all the manifestations of his divine presence with us. . . . God has now so signally displayed himself to our wondering eyes, that the pillar of cloud by day and of fire by night was not more plain to the children of Israel. He has smitten our enemies in their most tender and sensitive point, their invincible power, and has taken from us the pride of victory by giving it to us wrapped up in the funeral shroud of the brave and the young.[36]

Other preachers, likening the Confederate Army to that of Cromwell, declared, "We are a people saved by the Lord,"[37] and contended that "Unless the Lord had been on our side, they had swallowed us up quick. . . ."[38]

And so the same old theme was repeatedly voiced throughout the life of the Confederacy. A pleased God smiled on his people at Second Manassas, Fredericksburg, Chancellorsville, Chickamauga, and Cold Harbor, but turned his sterner side to them at Donelson, Malvern Hill, Gettysburg, Vicksburg, and Chattanooga. Apparently, it never occurred to anyone that He might have been a disinterested or even a disgruntled spectator.

Military leaders reflected religious sentiments of the people and, as every beginning student of the Civil War knows, Lee and Jackson were especially prone to give credit to the Lord for their victories. It was even more logical,

[36] *God's Presence with Our Army at Manassas* . . . (Savannah, 1861), pp. 7, 9.
[37] Moore, *op. cit.*, p. 14.
[38] Edward Reed, *A People Saved by the Lord* . . . (Charleston, 1861), p. 11. The Reverend C. A. Davis of the Cumberland Presbyterian Church, Memphis, assured his congregation that God and Right were on the side of the South. He compared the war to the American Revolution. The South was attacked by the North, Lincoln's election had repealed the Constitution; hence, the South was not fighting the Federal government, but only the usurpers of power. "While we can get anything else, we will never take upon us the reign of Abraham Lincoln" (Fred T. Wooten, "Religious Activities in Civil War Memphis," *Tennessee Historical Quarterly*, III, 135-136, June, 1944).

then, that the warrior bishop, General Leonidas Polk, in his report on his success at Belmont, should have acknowledged the favoring providence of Almighty God, who had unveiled the plans of the enemy and had strengthened Southern hearts in the day of battle. "He has given us the victory."[39]

Reverses in the winter and spring of 1862 presented the Southern people with a dreary prospect, but they were told that sooner or later God "will work out our deliverance. All the powers of earth and hell cannot prevent it, or delay it beyond his own appointed time."[40] And, indeed, with Lee hitting his stride in Virginia and with Grant bogged down in the West, Confederate fortunes improved enough to countenance two invasions of the North. The whole character of the war had been reversed—"an actual exhibition of Divine power in our successes," said the Reverend Mr. David S. Doggett. "Not only the preacher in his sermon, and the Christian at his prayers, but those unaccustomed to the exercises of piety, felt and acknowledged the hand of God." The Lord could not be an idle spectator: "He will not suffer public justice and integrity to struggle unaided in a never ceasing whirl of conflict with the elements of iniquity." With all material advantages on the side of the North, God must have intervened, overruling "the boasted arrangements of man, that he might vindicate the supremacy of his moral judgment."[41] J. M. Atkinson added that "God had good reason to send sorrow," but when sorrow had done its appointed work, "God poured his dauntless heroism into the hearts of a whole people. If our eyes could have been unsealed during those seven days [before Richmond] . . . we should have seen an angel, terrible as that which smote the host of Sennacherib, hurling back the multitudinous cohorts of our self confident invaders, filling their ranks with confusion, dismay, and death."[42]

[39] *General Polk's Report of the Battle of Belmont* (Columbus, Ky., 1861), p. 6.
[40] *Florida Sentinel* (Tallahassee), March 4, 1862.
[41] *A Nation's Ebenezer* . . . (Richmond, 1862), pp. 7-9.
[42] *God the Giver of Victory and Peace* . . . (Raleigh, 1862), pp. 5-7.

Stephen Elliott's exuberance allowed him to prophesy that "the summer's sun shall not have passed away, ere we shall find ourselves freed from their power." Speaking of the infidelity of Bostonians, he was sure the war would not end "until punishment shall have been rolled back upon the fountain of evil whence have sprung all these bitter waters," and although Confederate cannon might not reach them, "God is upon their track and ere this conflict is ended, will bring them to repentance and remorse or else punish them in the day of his wrath."[43] The Reverend J. H. Martin of Knoxville was willing "to give the glory and praise to God" for Southern victories, "but at the same time honorable mention may properly be made of those by whom they are wrought."[44] The Presbyterian Synod of Virginia stated that "At first God did not seem to smile on our defensive operations. . . . Then God put it into the heart of Davis to call for a day of fasting, humiliation, and prayer. . . . the united supplication of the whole people went up before the God of battles and was graciously accepted through the intercession of our great High Priest." The answer came almost at once—" . . . gloriously did God avenge his own elect. . . . We were wonderfully delivered out of the hands of our enemies."[45]

Early in 1863 the Baptist *Religious Herald* stated once more what the South was fighting for — "political and domestic institutions handed down from our fathers; for the sovereignty of the States, against a crushing central despotism; for the ascendancy of the master, against an infidel humanitarianism, which in the name of the Scripture disavows and villifies the scriptural sanction of hereditary service, and in the name of philanthropy casts an

[43] *Our Cause in Harmony with the Purposes of God in Christ Jesus* . . . (Savannah, 1862), pp. 22-23. The defeats in the West and the reason "Manassas went so strangely and mysteriously" unimproved rested on God's discipline of his people "for a more thorough Union with the South, and might bring them more heartily into the support of the institution he was protecting." Elliott warned, "Let us not, by any improper exultation, turn away God's wrath from our enemies. . . .

[44] *Christian Observer*, Sept. 18, 1862.

[45] *Minutes of the Synod of Virginia* . . . (Richmond, 1862), p. 314.

inferior race loose from that role which is also a protection. . . ." God had protracted the war until these principles
should become "avowedly so."[46]

A few months later the preachers were concentrating
their fire on "a deep and widespread yearning for peace."
According to Stephen Elliott, foreign intervention at this
time would be detrimental to the South because of Northern
occupation of much of its territory. "I firmly believe that
God has put it into the hearts of our enemies to reject it."
The only prospect was for continued war "which God is
working out for our deliverance"—might mean civil strife
in the United States or a rupture with Europe.[47] The Reverend Mr. James B. Ramsey took his text from the martyred
Jackson, who had told him in 1860: "Why should Christians
be at all disturbed about the dissolution of the Union? It can
only come by God's permission, and will only be permitted
if for his people's good, for does he not say all things shall
work together for good to them that love God?" The Lord
would not have given the Confederacy such a man "if he
had not designs of mercy for us, and was not preparing us
for a glorious deliverance. . . . Let the watchword of our
whole country in her present bloody struggle be 'Forward,
and remember Jackson.' "[48]

Bishop Pierce told the Georgia Assembly in March, 1863
that President Davis was well aware that cordial, earnest,
united supplication would secure divine blessing upon the
army and the administration. God's marvelous interven-
tions had convinced even the skeptical that the Lord "is for
us and with us." The attitude of the country had been
sublime:

With her foot planted on the right and her trust in God,
undismayed by numbers and armaments and navies, without
the sympathy of the world, shut in, cut off, alone, she has
battled through two long, weary years, gallantly, heroically,

[46] Jan. 29, 1863.
[47] "Samson's Riddle," A Sermon . . . (Macon, 1863), p. 13.
[48] True Eminence Found in Holiness . . . (Lynchburg, 1863), pp.
2, 21.

triumphantly, and today is stronger in men, resources, faith and hope than when Fort Sumter's proud flag was lowered in her maiden arms.   It is the Lord's doing, and it is marvelous in our eyes.[49]

The *Christian Observer* pointed out that April 30, 1863 had been observed in the North as a day of fasting and prayer.   Within a week Forrest whipped the Federals at Moulton, Alabama, the Yankees were repulsed at Grand Gulf, Chancellorsville had taken place, Federal boats had been burned at Vicksburg, and Hooker had begun his retreat.   "A retributive providence is often seen among men in the present life."[50]

After Vicksburg and Gettysburg there came an avalanche of sermons stressing the sins of the Confederate people. The *Church Intelligencer* questioned, "Are we to present ourselves before the Lord . . . with the secret purpose of still selling as dear as we can under some specious pretext? Do we expect God to hear us in such a frame of mind? For God's sake . . . let us pause and reflect! Do not let us insult and provoke the Majesty of Heaven and earth by a miserable, blasphemous mocking!"[51] The Lutheran Synod of South Carolina declared, "Our trust must still be in the God of battles, who has permitted us to suffer reverses that we may learn upon whose arm we should depend."[52] "It is a visitation of God," declared Bishop Elliott, "to make us understand that present victory and final success depend altogether upon his presence and his favor." Elliott's purpose was to recall the very high ground taken by the people two years before and to arouse its maintenance under all sacrifices.   A day of gloom had unexpectedly settled over the land—the people were conscious that "our hands hang down and that our knees are feeble."   Paralysis must be lifted from the South's heart where it rested like a weight

[49] *Sermons of Bishop Pierce and Rev. B. M. Palmer*, p. 5.

[50] May 28, 1863.

[51] Dec. 4, 1863.

[52] *Minutes of the Evangelical Lutheran Synod and Ministerium of South Carolina* . . . (Columbia, 1864), p. 6.

of lead, placed there by the Lord. There had been no rally from recent shocks. God was trying the South.

The earth mourneth and languisheth. Lebanon is ashamed and hewn down. Sharon is like a wilderness. They that did feel delicately are desolate in the streets; they that were brought up in scarlet embrace dunghills. They ravished the women in Zion and the maids in the streets of Judah. They took the young men to grind, and the children fell under the wood. The joy of our heart is ceased; our dance is turned into mourning. The crown is fallen from our head—woe unto us that we have sinned.[53]

Effective or not, these words were designed to rekindle the sacred fires of patriotism.

Dr. Palmer exulted before the South Carolina legislature that the "language of true prayer is never the cry of supine imbecility, nor the wail of craven despondency. It is always the language of hope and expectation.... I thank God that, in the darkest hour, I have never despaired of the republic."[54] LeRoy M. Lee warned his Lynchburg congregation of "speculators, forestallers, and extortioners,—if we would escape extermination ... there remaineth nothing but war —fierce, bloody, portracted war."[55] But it remained for Dr. Joseph C. Stiles to flourish the bravest "Appeal to the Confederate States."

Oh, how far you live from the light! Why, let the North march out her million of men on the *left*, and array upon the *right* all the veteran troops of England, France, Russia and Austria; and bring up the very gates of hell in all their strength to compose the *centre* of her grand invading army. What then? Why, *everything in God and from God assures us* that these Confederate States would hear a voice from heaven: "The battle is not yours but mine. Stand ye still and see the salvation of the Lord." If they dared to advance

---

[53] *Ezra's Dilemma* ... (Savannah, 1863), pp. 6, 25.
[54] *A Discourse before the General Assembly of South Carolina* ... (Columbia, 1864), p. 20.
[55] *Our Country—Our Dangers—Our Duty* ... (Richmond, 1863), p. 11.

one step, a righteous and an angry God would fire off upon the aliens terrible thunder that angel ears never heard, and shoot out upon them vengeful fires and lightnings that cherubic vision never saw, and fling down upon them cataracts of angry power that hell herself never felt, and if necessary to our deliverance, shake the very earth from under their feet.[56]

Just before Christmas, 1863 the editor of the *Chronicle and Sentinel* noted that a high Confederate official had confessed to a friend that, "We are whipped." He thought that such an opinion would cause "widespread demoralization," and should not be admitted, even if it were true. "If we believe our cause is just, then to cry whipped is to be an infidel," because God was with the Confederacy.[57]

In the spring and summer of 1864 there came a resurgence of hope and expectancy in the South. The Georgia Baptists, recognizing the futility of help from abroad, declared ". . . it is better to trust in the Lord than to put confidence in princes . . . if the God of Heaven shall recognize us, all shall be well."[58] Bishop Richard H. Wilmer, admitting that reverses had caused many to lose heart, contended they were "a part of our discipline . . . a part of our heritage." Comparing the situation to the dark days of the Revolution, he was sure that God would achieve the work in hand "in His own good time," but "To die for one's country is becoming, is beautiful."[59] Many were the versions that went the rounds about the last visit of General Lee to Bishop Meade. One stated that the dying bishop, placing his hands on Lee's head, had said, "You are engaged in a holy cause—the cause of Liberty—the cause of unborn millions. You are a Christian soldier. God thus far owns and blesses you. . . . Trust in God, Gen. Lee, with all your heart . . . you will never be

56 *National Rectitude the Only True Basis of National Prosperity: An Appeal to the Confederate States* (Petersburg, 1863), p. 43.

57 Dec. 20, 1863.

58 [S. Boykin], *History of the Baptist Denomination in Georgia* (Atlanta, 1881), p. 235.

59 *Future Good—The Explanation of Present Reverses* . . . (Charlotte, 1864), p. 24.

overcome."[60]   The Reverend Mr. Charles Minnigerode declared that God "chooseth his people in the furnace of affliction.   He who believeth . . . cannot become the plaything of every puff of adversity or prosperity.   What we need is a *stout heart* and a *firm, settled mind*: and oh! may we as a NATION remember, 'he that believeth shall not make haste.' "   He continued:

Oh, if we could take with us into the new year the lesson of our text; if we could stop every croaker and nerve every patriot; if we could allay every impatience and rouse all to bear what others have borne, and drive away their unmanly fears by trusting in God, . . . and urge them TO DO AND BEAR, to brave their dangers and endure their privation, . . . the threatening dangers . . . would be changed into blessings, and this year witness the growth of our national strength and our training for the final victory!   Let us confess it brethren, there has been no nation which has started her career . . . with such boastfulness and looked upon her struggles as so transient, her victory as so easily achieved, as ours. . . . let us do our duty as in His sight . . . and we cannot, we shall never fail![61]

In the fall of 1864 the *Christian Observer* printed statements emphasizing the "Sufferings of Our Enemies," "Anarchy in East Tennessee," the "Waste of Human Life" (showing Grant's losses), the "Barbarous Inhumanity" of the Yankees, and deprecating reports on the treatment of Northern prisoners in the South.   With every issue came the implication that sooner or later God would take care of

[60] Lynchburg (Va.) *Weekly Register*, April 9, 1864.   From this story the moral: "Tell me not ye skeptics that it is enthusiasm, when I boldly assert that I firmly believe that by that act of Bishop Meade, Gen. Lee was rendered invincible.   The dying blessings of that holy man will rest upon him throughout the war.   Federal millions may hawl for his destruction, and all the blood hounds from Lincoln's kennel may be turned loose to hunt him down.   Rivers of blood may be shed, and thousands of lives sacrificed . . . but amidst all the carnage and blood . . . Gen. Lee, as with charmed life, will stand secure."

[61] "*He that believeth shall not make haste* . . . "   (Richmond, 1865), pp. 8-13.

his people.[62]   Joseph Cross reminded the South that Joshua's warriors had been armed from the enemy; "And were not the victorious Hebrews vastly outnumbered by the Yankees of the desert?"[63]   Still hopeful, the Raleigh *Church Intelligencer* believed that "life, liberty, honour, property, and all else that makes this world worth living in, are suspended over a gulf of unfathomable degradation, which a breath of displeasure from the nostrils of God, may consign to unutterable and inconceivable ruin; but which His smile of favour will guard and preserve, and eventually restore to peace and safety."[64]

The understatement of 1864 came from Virginia Presbyterians, aware that the afflictive judgment of God was pressing heavily upon the church.   In its narrative of the state of religion, the Synod, grateful that "we are enabled at all to live and to labor," would also make mention of the solemn truth—"that amid all our blessings and mercies—God has most sorely afflicted us."[65]

Until Appomattox the church and its leaders waited patiently for God to strike down the infidels from the North.   In January, 1865, for instance, Dr. David Shaver, editor of the *Religious Herald,* declared: "If a feeling of despondency with regard to the struggle for Southern Independence, has gone abroad among our people, we do not share it."   He did not for one instant doubt that if the people would come before the throne of grace in the spirit of prayer, the "Chastening Hand of God shall be turned against our enemies, and His Protecting Hand shall cover us."[66]   His paper was burned in the Richmond fire.

---

[62] Other headings for editorials and news items: "Avarice Our National Sin," "The Dark Days of the Revolution," "Glorying in Tribulations," "Trials of the North," "Brutal Outrages of the Enemy," "Life under Military Despotism," "The Greed of Gain," "Spirit of the Northern Pulpit," and "The Hand of God in War."

[63] *Camp and Field: Papers from the Portfolio of an Army Chaplain* (Macon, 1864), III, 156-188.

[64] Nov. 16, 1864.

[65] Minutes of the Lexington Presbytery, 1860-1865 (MS, in Union Theological Seminary, Richmond), p. 362.

[66] March 16, 1865.

On June 18, 1865 John H. Caldwell preached at Newnan, Georgia, a sermon entitled, "The Slavery Conflict and Its Effect on the Church." Acknowledging that he had ever been convinced that there were many, many things wrong with slavery but that no minister would have been permitted by the slave power to speak out against them, the Reverend Mr. Caldwell came to a logical conclusion: "If the institution of slavery had been right, God would not have suffered it to be overthrown. . . ."[67]

The church had eaten its cake, and had it too.

[67] *Slavery and Southern Methodism . . .* (Newnan, 1865), p. iii.

Chapter III

The Church Will Sound the Trumpets

For those Southerners who believed they were God's chosen people and that the Confederacy was a part of God's plan, it was a matter of simple semantics to identify religion with politics and patriotism. As children of the Lord they were obviously under heavy obligation to support with enthusiasm the government and the war. The flesh of frail humans, however, was certain to prove weak and faltering unless sustained and encouraged by acknowledged leaders of the people. Politicians, newspaper editors, and men of military reputation all had their adherents but in time of crisis only the men of God could count on an almost universal hearing. Morale was a thing of the spirit.

A solemn ritual soon developed in the publication of Confederate sermons.[1] On a Sunday afternoon a special committee of prominent members from the congregation called unexpectedly at the parish house to inquire whether the minister would consent to have his message printed. Invariably he modestly protested that his words were hardly worthy of such honor but that (after a few moments of proper indecision), if the committee really felt they might do the cause of God and the Confederacy some good, he would revise them and allow them to go to press.

For instance, when Benjamin M. Palmer was asked for a copy of his sermon, "The Rainbow Round the Throne," he confessed that he would have to write it out since it had

---

[1] The author has examined well over a hundred Confederate sermons.

been prepared in great haste and he had not a single note of its contents.[2]   Bishop Elliott's wardens and vestrymen requested the publication of one of his pastoral discourses, "believing that the views presented are eminently calculated to further the cause of the Confederacy."[3]   The Reverend Mr. J. J. D. Renfroe frankly dedicated his remarks to the common people with the devout prayer that God "will teach their fingers to fight" the battles of liberty, their tongues to speak for the defence of their country, and their souls to supplicate the throne for grace, peace, and independence.[4] On occasion state legislatures and even troops in the field defrayed the publication costs of particularly effective sermons.[5]

Bishop Green was visibly concerned by the use of the church for war-like purposes. On June 17, 1863 he preached in St. Andrew's Church in Jackson, Mississippi, but had good reason to fear that the effect of the sermon was utterly driven from the minds of the congregation by the unseemly manner in which the organ was played at the close of the service—"the harsh and martial style of the music being much better suited to a military parade than to the quiet solemnity of the House of God."   This was not the first time, for in other places "have I seen congregations just rising from their knees under the Priestly benediction, marching out of the Church to the notes of some warlike air, well calculated to inspire any other feeling than that of devotion."[6]   Likewise, the Baptist Association at Columbus,

---

[2] Quoted in DesChamps, *op. cit.*, XIX, 21 (Sept., 1953).

[3] *"Samson's Riddle,"* p. 2.

[4] *"The Battle is God's"* . . . (Richmond, 1863), pp. 2-3. The Reverend Mr. Doggett's *The War and Its Close* . . . (Richmond, 1864) was published "by request," that it might be "a witness to the truth, an incentive to duty, and a stimulant to hope in the present stage of our country's fortunes."

[5] *Acts of the General Assembly of the State of Georgia . . . 1862*, and *Extra Session of 1863* (Milledgeville, 1863), p. 239. Two thousand copies of the March 27, 1863 sermons of Bishop Pierce and Dr. Palmer were published, as were 2,000 copies of sermons in December, 1863 by "Drs. Higgins and Marshall."   On one occasion, soldiers raised $360 to pay for the publication of a sermon by the Reverend A. E. Dickinson (*Religious Herald*, Sept. 17, 1863).

[6] *Journal of the Protestant Episcopal Convention, Diocese of Mississippi* (Jackson, 1865), p. 7.

Georgia, was extremely critical of the conduct of its ministry for having preached war from the social circle and from the pulpit—they "have been exercised more by the war spirit than by the spirit of the Gospel."[7]

The Episcopalian Council in Virginia was convinced that "what is wanted, is not sermons on the times and the war and the objects of the country's hopes," but "just the glad tidings of salvation."[8]   The *Christian Observer,* however, more nearly expressed prevailing religious sentiment when it denied that the clergy could be neutral. "They might as well cease to pray for their daily bread, as to doubt the propriety of offering fervent prayer to God for the success of our arms and the discomfiture of our enemies."[9]   In official conclave Virginia Presbyterians, though concerned about "grinding the seed corn," approved the patriotic spirit which induced so many of the young men to volunteer.[10]

As early as February 27, 1861 the congregation of Charleston's Grace Church gained permission to publish Charles Cotesworth Pinckney's sermon in the hope that it "would add to the general good by giving proper direction to the thoughts of those engaged in establishing a Government . . . as well as in aiding the public mind to receive the efforts of their labor. . . ."   Pastor Pinckney was optimistic: "With that all pervading blessing to crown our work; with our acknowledged advantages, agricultural, commercial, social and religious, with a united people, walking in fear of the Lord, and the faith of the Gospel, we may expect to retain the favor of heaven."[11]

Shortly after Fort Sumter the Southern Baptist Convention, admonishing Northern preachers for "breathing out slaughter," resolved: (1) denial of the responsibility of the

[7] *Minutes of the Thirty-Fourth Annual Session of the Columbus Baptist Association* (Columbus, 1862), p. 13.

[8] *Journal of the Sixty-Eighth Annual Convention of the Protestant Episcopal Church in Virginia* . . .   (Richmond, 1863), p. 39.

[9] Aug. 14, 1862.

[10] *Minutes of the Synod of Virginia, at Their Session in Petersburg* . .   (Richmond, 1861), p. 284.

[11] *Nebuchadnezzar's Fault and Fall* . . .   (Charleston, 1861), pp. 13-14.

South for secession, (2) approval of the Confederate States, (3) invocation of divine blessing on the Confederacy's rulers, (4) expression of sympathy for the administration, (5) condemnation of the "lawless reign of terror" in the North, and "threats to wage upon the South a war of ruthless barbarity, to devastate our homes and hearths with hordes of ruffians and felons, burning with lust and rapine," (6) invocation of prayer for God to protect Southern soldiers, (7) supplication to the Lord for a change of heart in the enemy, (8) observance of fast days, and (9) sending of copies of the resolutions to President Davis and to the Congress.[12] Some two weeks later the Virginia Baptists, declaring that "our sons are valiant and would rather die than bend to oppression," went along with "all lawful and Christian means in the support of the government."[13]

In June, 1861 Stephen Elliott sent the Pulaski Guards off to war. "Ye may go to battle without any fear, and strike boldly for your homes and your altars without any guilt. . . . The church will sound the trumpets that shall summon you to the battle. . . .," he wrote.[14] On the first Confederate fast day he summed up the situation:

We are engaged in one of the grandest struggles which ever nerved the hearts or strengthened the hands of a heroic race. We are fighting for great principles, for sacred objects. . . . to prevent ourselves from being transferred from American republicanism to French democracy . . . to rescue the fair name of our social life . . . from dishonor . . . to protect and preserve a race who form a part of our household, and stand with us next to our children. . . . to

[12] *Minutes of the Baptist Convention of the State of Georgia, 1861* (Macon, 1861), p. 5. The report of a Committee on the State of the Nation began: "We hold these truths to be self-evident, that governments are established for the security, prosperity, and happiness of the people. When, therefore, any government is perverted from its proper design, becomes oppressive, and abuses its power, the people have a right to change it."
[13] *Minutes of the Baptist General Association of Virginia* (Petersburg, 1863), p. 16.
[14] *The Silver Trumpets of the Sanctuary* . . . (Savannah, 1861), p. 4.

drive away the infidel and rationalistic principles which are sweeping over the land and substituting a gospel of the stars and stripes for the gospel of Jesus Christ.[15]

On the same day J. R. Kendrick protested against this "most iniquitous and cruel" appeal to arms in which the Confederacy was forced to send "her sons to the red fields of war,"[16] and Thomas Smyth cried exultantly, "We have crossed swords with the Northern Confederacy over the Bible. What a spectacle to God, to angels, and to the world! What lamentation in heaven! What a jubilee in hell! What a triumph to despotism and infidelity." The Irish theologian continued with a wholesale indictment of the Lincoln government:

See how these Christians hate one another, and how Republicans, by a sectional minority, take the government out of the hands of a million majority, and put it into the hands of a military despotism; which sets aside the Supreme Court; tramples on the Constitution; ignores, and even opposes Congress; against all constitutional authority sets up Scott as a military dictator; calls for seventy-five thousand and accepts two hundred and fifty thousand troops; proclaims war; creates a self-chosen military Board to supercede State authorities; declares martial law; sets at defiance the fundamental right of *habeas corpus* and the decrees of Courts, even of the Supreme Court; abolishes trial by jury; not only raises armies, but orders their number and term of service, and compels them to take a test oath of allegiance; builds, purchases and hires ships of war; mans, equips, and gives them secret and peremptory orders; blockades ports of States still declared to be in the Union; divides such States into military districts; takes military possession of Maryland, against the declarations of her authorities; shoots down her citizens, forcibly seizes her arms, dwellings, and property; imprisons her citizens without charge or trial; establishes a hostile camp commanding Baltimore, and opens the batteries of Fort McHenry on the

---

[15] *God's Presence with the Confederate States* . . . (Savannah, 1861), pp. 20-21.
[16] *Discourses of Rev. J. R. Kendrick* (in Curry Pamphlets).

city; takes military possession of St. Louis, and shoots down men, women and children in her streets; foments and aids civil war in Virginia, Kentucky, Texas, and Missouri; invades Virginia, and takes military possession of Hampton and Alexandria, where it brutally murders a peaceful citizen defending his own house, family and property against an infamous soldiery who were permitted to rob and pillage an unarmed and unresisting population, and to outrage helpless women; has destroyed public property in ships, buildings and forts, to an amount of some twenty millions of dollars, and involved the country, even in the period of a few months, in a loss of not less than one thousand millions of dollars; which has justified the cowardly assassination of a resident citizen of Washington, at the door of his own house, to which he had been summoned for the coldblooded purpose of murder; hung, without trial, a merchant of Hampton, Virginia, for shooting an officer who took forcible possession of his store and goods, and struck him in the face with his drawn sword; stripped a gentleman of the same town stark naked, and in that condition marched him as a prisoner to Fortress Monroe; destroyed crops and houses, and other property, in a single county, and in a single week, to the extent of five hundred thousand dollars; commanded the retention of all fugitive slaves; attempted, through a slave cook to poison the food of the soldiery; plots the assassination of President Davis; violated all the confidential sanctities of the telegraph and post office; established a reign of terror, by a system of espionage and threats, over men and women, over the press and free speech, and against all law, human and divine; is now proceeding, unless God prevent, to carry devastation throughout the South, until it is brought into prostrate subjection; who privateers, while proclaiming it to be piracy and worthy of death; and who employs mercenary foreign hirelings to invade, ravage, and destroy unarmed and unsuspecting towns of a neutral State, shooting its inhabitants, and barbarously trampling and kicking to death an infirm old man, eighty years of age.[17]

Southern preachers of all denominations belched forth their fiery patriotic sermons for the rest of the war. In

[17] *The Battle of Fort Sumter: Its Mystery and Miracle: God's Mastery and Mercy* (Columbia, 1861), pp. 45-46.

July, 1861 Bishop Alexander Gregg told his congregation in Austin, Texas, that war was sometimes necessary and that patriotism was a virtue sanctioned by religion in such a war as this—"which threatens to crimson its mountain tops and make red its fairest valleys, to swell with human gore the ceaseless tide of the father of waters, and deluge this western continent with blood." From the *altar* of Southern patriotism, according to Gregg, was rising the incense of willing devotion of millions of hearts. Never had there been a purer, nobler emulation to discharge the last duty of a patriotic people in defending their heritage. With Southern support of the war assured, the bishop cried aloud to God: "*Stir up thy strength,* O Lord! and come and help us. . . ."[18] In August a Georgia Presbyterian convention called upon Southerners: "Up, quit you like men. Pour your treasures into the lap of your country; throw your stout arms around her; let her feel the tendrils of enduring affection around her heart; and, if need be, let your blood flow like water. . . . Put your trust in God, and pray your Country through this dreadful war."[19] In two issues of the *Central Presbyterian* appeared a long sermon by Reverend J. G. Shepperson of Bedford County, Virginia, entitled: "The Defence of Our Country a Christian Duty."[20] Catholic Bishops Patrick Lynch of Charleston, Elder of Natchez, and Martin of Natchitoches enthusiastically supported the Confederacy, but issued their pronouncements in less bombastic fashion.[21]

When the South began to settle down to the reality of a war of attrition, there was greater necessity for such admonitions as that of Stephen Elliott in November, 1861: "We are only at the beginning of a long and bloody conflict, and it is the duty of everyone to consider it so and prepare himself for such a contingency." He defended Davis's defen-

---

[18] *The Duties Growing Out of It, and The Benefits To Be Expected from the Present War* (Austin, 1861), p. 7; *A Few Historical Records of the Church in the Diocese of Texas . . .* (New York, 1865), p. 11.

[19] *Proceedings of a Convention of Delegates from Various Presbyteries in the Confederate States of America* (Atlanta, 1861), p. 13.

[20] Aug. 10, 1861.

[21] Blied, *op. cit.,* pp. 25, 67.

sive strategy, (it "demands a high degree of moral courage") and he castigated those guilty of the sin of destroying confidence in the government. "We are moving in the light of God's countenance, and the waving of His hand and the flashing of His eye are almost visible to us." There was no ground for despondency, for the Confederacy had moved forward majestically during 1861 and "God is dropping arms into our hands, as if from the skies, and our finances are not disordered."[22]

Admitting that the New Year of 1862 had not begun with its wonted gladness, Moses D. Hoge looked forward to a protracted struggle and called for UPRIGHT, PATRIOT STATEMEN whose example would lead to virtuous constituencies. The demand was urgent because only Christianity could fire the heart and nerve of the patriot soldier.[23]

In the spring, with the Confederacy apparently crumbling, the Union Baptist Association of Texas endorsed the course of the government and belligerently resolved:

. . . although their numbers may be legion, and they encompass us by land and sea, take our cities and destroy our towns, ascend our rivers with flotillas, confiscate our property and threaten us with the halter, slay many of our brave soldiers . . . prejudice foreign nations against us, issue disgraceful edicts against lovely and amiable women, yet none of these things move us, except to inspire us to a more unconquerable determination. . . . If need be, we will burn our cotton, spread destruction before the enemy, spend the last dollar, shed the last drop of blood, and be subjugated never! never! never![24]

Bishop Elliott reasoned that Confederate reverses had been necessary for purification but would stir up the energies of the people and would quell faction, break up party spirit and bring out patriotism, valor, self-denial, and heroism.

---

[22] *How to Renew Our National Strength* . . . (Savannah, 1861), pp. 6, 14.

[23] *The Christian Statesman* . . . (Richmond, 1862), p. 7.

[24] J. M. Carroll, *A History of the Texas Baptists* . . . (Dallas, 1923), pp. 318-319.

True enough, these were worldly virtues but they would supplant selfishness and avarice.[25] After the situation improved, the same pattern remained in religious proclamations. In June Bishop Gregg urged his people "to move on with unwavering fortitude,"[26] and the *Florida Sentinel* reported a Nashville sermon in which the Reverend S. D. Baldwin predicted that the great battle of Armageddon would be fought within a fortnight, with the Federal hosts overthrown and dispersed, their dead carcasses making "all the land to stink."[27] That fall North Carolina Presbyterians requested increasing prayer "that the Lord God may be as a wall of fire about our land; that the Angel of the covenant may go forth as the Captain of our hosts."[28]

Before the spring campaigns of 1863 had got underway, Rabbi M. J. Michelbacher of Richmond published a sermon in which he categorically defended Jews from vicious charges of extortion and suggested that the Israelite did not need the persuasion of conscription because he had never failed to defend his native land. Addressing himself to "the Great and terrible Lord of the universe," the rabbi implored: " . . . even now, *Thou dost call upon the people of the South in the words Thou gavest to Nehemiah*: '*Fight for your brethren, your sons, and your daughters, your wives and your houses!*' *Who will turn a deaf ear to this Heavenly command . . . ?*" God had promised to protect him who defended himself, his home, and his family from a public enemy.[29]

On April 30, 1863 ninety-six ministers of all faiths issued an "Address to Christians Throughout the World," which was published widely in the Confederacy. From "no political source whatever," this lengthy document ably argued that (1) the North could not possibly accomplish its

[25] "*New Wine not to Be Put in Old Bottles*," p. 17.

[26] *Journal of the 13th Annual Convention of the Protestant Episcopal Church in Diocese of Texas*, p. 32.

[27] June 10, 1862.

[28] *Minutes of the Forty-Nineth* [sic] *Sessions of the Synod of North Carolina* (Fayetteville, 1863), p. 17.

[29] *A Sermon Delivered . . . at the German Hebrew Synagogue,* "*Bayth Ahabah.*" (Richmond, 1863), p. 9.

desires by force, (2) Southern people were determined that separation was final, (3) emancipation should be solemnly protested against by all Christians, (4) the war had produced only evil results, and (5) the moral and religious views of the South ought to be appreciated by all Christians.[30]

As usual, the prolific Thomas Smyth was among the most pronounced zealots in the pulpit. In the April, 1863 issue of the *Southern Presbyterian Review*, he declared "The War of the South Vindicated" (1) in self-defence, (2) by fundamental principles of American liberty, (3) as a defensive struggle against fanatical abolition, and (4) by the "divine right" of secession. The North was guilty of "treasonable rebellion" against the world, Providence, and government of God. Having established his general thesis, Dr. Smyth proceeded with the exhortation:

Let the spirit of resistance be infused, with its mother's milk, into the baby in its cradle. Let it mingle with the plays of childhood. Let it animate the boy in its mimic manhood; the maiden in the exercise of her magic, spellbinding influence; the betrothed in her soul-subduing trance of hope and memory; the bride at the altar; the wife in the arms of her rejoicing husband; the young mother amid the whirl of ecstatic joy; the matron in the bosom of her admiring children; and the father as he dreams fondly of the fortune and glory of his aspiring sons—let it fire the man of business at his place of merchandise; the lawyer among his briefs; the mechanic in his workshop; the planter in his fields; the laborer as he plies his pruning hook and follows his plough,—*let the trumpet blow in Zion, and let all her watchmen lift up their voice*;—let all the people, everywhere, old and young, bond and free, *take up the war-cry*, and say, each to his neighbor, "Gather ye together, and come against them, and rise up to the battle."[31]

---

[30] *Address to Christians Throughout the World. By the Clergy of the Confederate States of America* (London, 1863), pp. 1, 7; *Religious Herald*, April 30, 1863.

[31] Quoted in Stanton, *op. cit.*, pp. 171-173.

A curious bit of reasoning was put forth by the Reverend Mr. Watson, who denied that the war had been brought on by blood-thirsty harangues from Southern pulpits and that the Confederate church had "been degraded into arenas . . . for the venting of bitterness towards those she hopes to conquer," but who did argue that in such a religious war the church with clear conscience "can take her stand by the side of her battling children," and can send the "soldier to the field, as a part of God's work. . . ."[32] This attitude was quite similar to one expressed a few weeks earlier in a column in the *Christian Observer*. According to Dr. Ross, the preacher should speak the truth for his country, "and from the place where he has the highest power of influence."[33]

The peripatetic Palmer closed the year with a discourse before the South Carolina legislature in which he used the text, "O! God thou hast cast us off; thou hast scattered us, thou hast been displeased: O! turn thyself to us again. Thou hast made the earth to tremble; thou hast broken it; heal the breaches thereof, for it shaketh. Thou hast shown the people hard things; thou hast made us to drink the wine of astonishment; thou hast given a banner to them that feared thee, that it may be displayed because of the truth." But Palmer insisted that only a madman would cherish reconstruction and once again he thanked God that he had never despaired of the cause.[34]

On the first day of 1864 the *Army and Navy Messenger* of Petersburg, Virginia, aware that the people must be taught the crowning glory of endurance, suggested a program for the reassembled Congress. First of all, this church paper was pleased that Congress had already abolished substitution, whereby "a man was enabled to sell a negro, a bale of cotton or barrel of whiskey, buy a white man, and thus remain at home to acquire a fabulous fortune." Its proposal called for: (1) the revocation of details, (2) en-

---

[32] *Church Intelligencer*, June 26, 1863.
[33] May 21, 1863.
[34] *A Discourse Before the General Assembly of South Carolina*, pp. 3, 5.

listment of youthful tax collectors and other bureaucrats, (3) enrollment of refugees from the United States or Europe or "expedite the departure of so many consumers and extortioners. . . ," (4) conscription of all vagabonds, black-legs, pimps, and *sans-culottes* of the cities (plug-uglies, garroters and blood-tubs, admirable "food for pow-der," who ought to be fond of martial exercises), and (5) arrest of all deserters and skulkers.[35] These suggestions would have been insulting to the volunteers of 1861, but times had changed. Further proof of change could have been found in the columns of the *Religious Herald* which ran a series of editorials on the terrible things that had happened to churches in occupied territory. It abhorred the notion of submission and demanded war until independence or death had been achieved.[36]

Throughout 1864 preachers called for a return to Christ as the means of putting the Confederacy back on the road to victory. More than ever they tended to minimize defeat and to exaggerate the importance of minor Confederate successes. There was a sense of optimism, too, as in the as-sumption of the quotable Elliott, that the year would bring the last great effort to subdue the South. All that was needed was for the people to come "boldly up to the throne of Grace, firmly believing that our prayers . . . will return to us laden with blessings from . . . the God of the Armies of Israel." He spoke of the power left in the Confederacy, claimed that the original seceding states had hardly been touched, saw despondency in the North and an abundance of war materials in the South, and cracked down on South-ern murmuring about worldly sacrifices. Perhaps uncon-sciously, the bishop sensed the South's greatest weakness when he declared, " . . . freedom's battle will never go down in blood and disaster, unless the blows which destroy her come from within. . . ."[37]

[35] This paper was published to circulate the "pure word of God," under the auspices of the Evangelical Society of Petersburg.
[36] March 3, 1864.
[37] *A Sermon Preached in Christ Church, Savannah . . . April, 1864* (Macon, 1864), pp. 5, 18.

In May the *Christian Observer* magnified victories of Taylor, Price, and Smith in Louisiana. It quoted the Atlanta [Memphis] *Appeal* which had boasted that this territory wrested from Union troops was but the return wave flowing back upon the North, "and no earthly power can stay its progress." The entire South would soon be redeemed from the despotic tread of the Yankee invader.[38] A month later the Richmond paper noted a series of patriotic resolutions passed by the Baptist General Association in Virginia,[39] and later still it decried General Grant's alleged brutality in his apparently hopeless fight for Richmond.[40]

After the fall of Atlanta Stephen Elliott, rising to great heights in a dramatic appeal to patriotism, sounded the alarm: "We have nothing left but to follow the example of the Psalmist and crying unto God to 'give up help from trouble,' to acknowledge that 'vain is the help of man.' "[41] About the same time Mrs. Chesnut, returning from a Palmer discourse, confided in her diary: "What a sermon! The preacher stirred my blood. My very flesh crept and tingled. A red-hot glow of patriotism passed through me. Such a sermon must strengthen the hearts and the hands of many people. There was more exhortation to fight and die, *à la* Joshua, than meek Christianity."[42]

As Sherman swung through Georgia, the *Christian Index* admonished the country on "Duties of the Hour." The existence of the nation was at stake and its citizens must rally, even to the death. The whole people should arouse as one man: "Let the timid be brave, let the hesitating be decided, let croakers take heart, let the doubtful be reassured, let all be bold, confident, cheerful, laborious, self-sacrificing, and success will soon be ours."[43] At Thanksgiving time a pastoral letter went out to the Presbyterian

[38] May 26, 1864.
[39] June 9, 1864.
[40] June 23, 1864.
[41] *"Vain Is the Help of Man . . ."* (Macon, 1864), p. 4.
[42] Mary Boykin Chesnut, *A Diary From Dixie* (New York, 1905), p. 326.
[43] Quoted in *Christian Observer*, Oct. 20, 1864.

churches of Virginia calling on each citizen to labor on that part of the walls of Jerusalem before him.[44]

Though much of despair and despondency may be found in sermons in the waning months of the Confederacy, there is overwhelming evidence that preachers as a whole retained a higher degree of morale than they were able to instill into their parishioners. President Davis's pastor, the Reverend Dr. Minnigerode, on the first day of 1865 called for patience, calmness, and self possession: "He who believeth . . . cannot become the plaything of every puff of adversity or prosperity." The people desperately needed to rally on that faith which alone could see them through, he added. The day of miracles was past, but as the Romans had survived Lake Trasimene and Cannae, the Confederacy "cannot, we shall not fail."[45] In February Dr. Porter, of the Charleston Church of the Holy Communion, called upon his congregation to "Fight! fight, my friends, till the streets run blood! Perish in the last ditch rather than permit the enemy to obtain possession of your homes."[46] As late as March ministers of all denominations in Virginia were in the field, addressing the people in an effort to encourage moral firmness and support of the war. Jefferson Davis, in a coded message sent by way of Howell Cobb, requested Bishop Pierce to speak to the citizens of Georgia "and assure them that if they will do their duty all will be well. The faith of the country must not give way."[47] The President of the Confederacy well knew that any revival of the exhausted people of the South would have to come through their spiritual leaders.

One stratagem used widely throughout the conflict consisted of the exploitation of martyred heroes from obscure

---

[44] *Ibid.*, Nov. 24, 1864.

[45] *Op. cit.*, p. 13.

[46] Quoted in Charles C. Coffin, *Four Years of Fighting* . . . (Boston, 1866), p. 477.

[47] William A. Smith and James A. Duncan to General Howell Cobb, March 1, 1865, in *War of the Rebellion: A Compilation of the Official Records of the Union and Confederate Armies* (Washington, 1880-1891), 4 series, III, 1118.

privates to Stonewall Jackson and Leonidas Polk. On October 26, 1862 the Reverend W. D. Moore eulogized in a rather subdued funeral sermon the Mississippi sociologist, Henry Hughes. Author of a treatise in which he had defended slavery on the theoretical basis of "warranteeism," Hughes had enlisted as a private, had fought through Sharpsburg, and then had returned home to raise a band of partisan rangers to protect Claiborne and adjoining counties. Moore's appeal to patriotism came by indirection but probably was the more effective for that approach.[48] In a sermon commemorative of "The Christian Soldier," Phram Carrington, R. L. Dabney raised the "new argument for consecrating ourselves to our country's cause." To sustain the government with *heart* and *hand* had been ordered by God not only as a privilege but as a duty. Carrington's courage reflected the spirit with which his Divine Master had set his face steadfastly toward Jerusalem. The blood of Confederate dead would cry out from the ground, "if we permitted the soil which drank the precious libation to be polluted with the despot's foot. . . . before God, I take you to witness this day that this blood seals upon you the obligation to fill their places in your country's host. . . ."[49]

Feeling that such examples of devotion to religion and patriotism ought to be preserved for the benefit of the living, Nathaniel D. Renfroe paid tribute in January, 1863 to "A Model Confederate Soldier." Just before he was killed the hero from Atlanta had confided in his brother regarding the hardships of a barefoot volunteer but had submitted without a murmur "in view of my country's freedom and the honor of my religion."[50]

Dabney Harrison fell at Fort Donelson "while cheering on his men, and striking for the honor and independence of our young Confederacy." Harrison, himself a preacher, had watched the encroachments of Northern fanaticism "trampling on the Bible and the Constitution, cursing men

[48] *The Life and Works of Col. Henry Hughes; A Funeral Sermon . . .* (Mobile, 1863).

[49] *The Christian Soldier* (Richmond, 1862), p. 13.

[50] *A Model Confederate Soldier* (Richmond, 1863), p. 2.

and blaspheming God . . . with its eyes of greed, its brow of brass, its lips dripping with vemon, and its hands only not yet dripping with blood." His eulogist continued:

With reverence I have in my hand the hat he wore in battle. It is pierced by four balls. . . . His face was to the foe, and his step forward, even when . . . he sank to the frozen ground. . . . The blood of our fallen patriots consecrates the cause and the soil. To yield would be treason to the dead.[51]

In quite the same fashion the Reverend Mr. Joseph C. Stiles used his funeral sermon for Thomas E. King, wounded at Manassas and killed at Chickamauga, as a means for lashing out against speculators and deserters.[52] More than two weeks after he fell at Pine Mountain in June, 1864 Bishop-General Polk was buried in Augusta. Stephen Elliott's funeral sermon, published in the fall as "An Impressive Summons," included an unflattering commentary on Northern Christians and "the ripening germs of irreligion, of unbelief, of ungodliness, of corruption, of cruelty, of license which have distinguished them." Elliott's "murdered brother" would be returned to Louisiana with the success of the Confederacy.

That day will come; I see it rise before me in vision, when this martyred dust shall be carried in triumphal procession to his own beloved . . . diocese rescued from brutal domination by the efficacy of his blood! a church freed from pollution by the vigor of his counsels! — a country made independent through his devotion and self sacrifice.[53]

Most of the thousands of tiny tracts passed out to Confederate soldiers (twenty-six million copies were distributed by the fall of 1863[54]) were devoted to salvation and similar

---

[51] William J. Hoge, *Sketch of Dabney Carr Harrison* . . . (Richmond, 1863), pp. 16, 41, 45-46.
[52] *Capt. Thomas E. King: or, A Word to the Army and the Country* (Charleston, 1864).
[53] *Funeral Services at the Burial of the Right Rev. Leonidas Polk* . . . (Columbia, 1864), p. 17.
[54] Mobile (Ala.) *Register and Advertiser*, Oct. 20, 1863.

subjects, but at least a hundred contained unvarnished emotional appeals for patriotism. These, of course, were as effective with civilians as soldiers. Just before the spring campaigns of 1864, the *Army and Navy Messenger* announced the publication of another edition of one of these tracts, written by Dr. Thornwell, now dead, whose "stirring words, like the blast of a bugle, still echo through the land. We can conquer and we must. We can make every pass a Thermopylae, every street a Salamis, and every plain a Marathon. If we are overrun, we can at least die; and if our enemies possess our land, we can leave it a howling wilderness. But under God we shall not fail."[55]

Denominational quarterlies were directed mainly to clerical and lay leaders, but the religious weekly press was undoubtedly more influential with the reading public than secular newspapers.[56] Dr. Summers wrote to the *Southern Advocate* in May, 1862: "Patriotism is to be wedded to piety, and who but God's ministers are to perform the service? . . . every minister will have to be, as it were, a chaplain in the army, mixing, perhaps, not a little gunpowder with the Gospel."[57] Many of God's ministers were editors as well. The Nashville *Christian Advocate* claimed that the denominational press was as able as the secular press and printed war news because readers demanded it. As a matter of fact, according to the *Advocate*, the religious press had done more than its secular rival "to shape the course and quicken the patriotism of the Southern Confederacy." It had been ahead of the politicians in denouncing abolition and had infused into public movements the spirit of morality. "They have done much to make it a holy war, and thus far to insure its success." The large circulation of church papers augured well for their influence in shaping opinion and sentiment in the Confederacy.[58]

[55] April 1, 1864.
[56] *Central Presbyterian*, Jan. 4, 1862.
[57] Erasmus Q. Fuller (ed.), *An Appeal to the Records* . . . (Cincinnati, 1876), p. 276.
[58] Quoted in *Central Presbyterian*, Jan. 4, 1862.

The *Southern Lutheran*, noting that religious papers had "wheeled into line" very early, was pleased at their spirit of patriotic devotion. The press was wielding a powerful and controlling influence in its noble battle for church and country.[59] Always co-operative in publicizing days of prayer, the *Central Presbyterian* remained fairly objective in its battle reporting, "withholding nothing, concealing nothing," because the editors believed the people would "display the right spirit under these discomfitures."[60] It also ran stories about distress in the North and atrocities committed by Union troops, and carried war-like sermons. There were many references to the "Second American Revolution," with appropriate allusions to Washington and other Southern patriots. This paper was representative of the religious press.

Episcopalians meeting at Holly Springs, Mississippi in April, 1861 resolved that the secretary should extract the political remarks from the bishop's address, "and have the same published in at least one of the secular papers in each of the principal cities of this state," with the request that all religious papers would copy.[61] The *Christian Observer*, which ran countless supposedly morale-boosting stories on everything from bizarre historical parallels to attacks on Mrs. Lincoln, truthfully stated, as late as February, 1865, that the religious press had spoken "with remarkable unanimity of the duties required in the present crisis of our country."[62] Like the preachers, the editors never seemed to lose faith in the notion that God would come to the aid of his chosen people once He had thoroughly tested them.

Despite powerful though unorganized campaigns to unify the South, the Confederacy was not long in showing signs of internal dissension which eventually led to the people's loss of the resolution to win. The finger of blame had long been pointed accusingly at politicians Alexander Stephens

---

[59] Quoted in *Christian Observer*, Jan. 23, 1862.
[60] March 6, 1862.
[61] *Journal of the Thirty-Fifth Annual Convention of the Protestant Episcopal Church in the Diocese of Mississippi* (Jackson, 1861), p. 11.
[62] Feb. 9, 1865.

and Joseph E. Brown and editors of the Richmond *Examiner*, the Raleigh *Standard*, and the Charleston *Mercury*.[63] Indeed, it is an established fact that the Davis administration failed to receive the political and editorial support necessary for the Confederacy to present to the enemy a united front.

Perhaps because of the avowed piety of the highest civil and military leaders, the church gave the Richmond government its unfailing blessing. Fusion of church and state may be illustrated by Bishop Polk's call for support of the new administration "not only with material aid and personal services, but in supplication and prayer,"[64] and the claim made by the *Church Intelligencer* that the Louisiana bishop had been appointed a major general because of his great moral influence in the whole southwestern area.[65]

Before Alabama's secession Bishop Quinlan of Mobile wrote in a pastoral letter of the necessity of obedience to the highest recognized civil authority;[66] his support of the Davis administration continued throughout the war and as late as 1864 he was confident of Confederate success. In 1860 Alabama Baptists held themselves subject to the call of proper authority in defense of the sovereignty and independence of the state and her sacred right to leave the Union — "AND IN THIS DECLARATION WE ARE HEARTILY, DELIBERATELY, UNANIMOUSLY AND SOLEMNLY UNITED."[67] A year later the Southern Baptist Convention adopted resolutions, pledging enthusiastic support of the government, and the East Alabama Convention unanimously approved the administration and the war.[68]

---

[63] The *Religious Herald*, July 16, 1863, scored Edward A. Pollard, editor of the *Examiner*, for daring to criticize the Confederate government in his book, *The Second Year of the War* (Richmond, 1863).

[64] *Journal of the Twenty-Third Annual Convention of the Protestant Episcopal Church in the Diocese of Louisiana* . . . (New Orleans, 1861), p. 30.

[65] Sept. 14, 1864.

[66] Blied, *op. cit.*, pp. 59-60.

[67] Walter L. Fleming, "The Churches of Alabama During the Civil War and Reconstruction," *Gulf States Historical Magazine*, I, 105-127 (July, 1902).

[68] *Proceedings of the Southern Baptist Convention* . . . *May 10-13, 1861*, p. 63.

The *Southern Episcopalian* of March, 1861 featured a poem to Jefferson Davis, "O Chosen Leader in the Course of Right," and called for a united Southern church. Georgia Baptists resolved approval, endorsement, and support of the government and declared they would be behind no group in maintaining the independence of the South.[69]   In April, 1861 Bishop Green declared that secession had come *"with good cause"* and that the duty of patriot-churchmen "is not only to pray for the new government and rulers under whose authority we this day find ourselves, but to uphold with heart and hand the Constitution and Laws which our representatives have modelled for our guidance and protection." He was sure no son of the church would deny any call which the country might make on him.[70]   The *Central Presbyterian* declared of the administration: "Its support will be accepted as a religious trust."[71]   North Carolina Episcopalians saw the state as entitled to prayers and obedience "unless she undertakes to set aside the law of Christ. . . ."[72]   And in November, 1861 the Methodist Rio Grande Mission Conference resolved "that the government of the Confederate States of America is right; to it we owe allegiance, and its fortunes we share, invoking Almighty God to uphold it in equity and wisdom."[73]

After Seven Pines the Reverend George Woodbridge preached faith in Davis: "Whatever has a tendency to destroy public confidence in [the leaders'] prudence, their wisdom, their energy, their patriotism, undermines our cause."[74]   The *Army and Navy Messenger* was uniformly warlike in tone and favorable to the administration.[75]   In

[69] Boykin, *op. cit.*, p. 228; *Minutes of the Baptist Convention of the State of Georgia, 1861.*

[70] *Journal of the Thirty-Fifth Annual Convention, of the Protestant Episcopal Church in the Diocese of Mississippi*, pp. 64-65.

[71] Quoted in Stanton, *op. cit.*, pp. 186-187.

[72] *Journal of the Forty-Fifth Annual Convention of the Protestant Episcopal Church in the State of North Carolina* . . . (n.p., 1862), p. 15.

[73] Journal of the Rio Grande Mission Conference, 1859-1865 (MS, in University of Texas Library, Austin), p. 58.

[74] Richmond (Va.) *Enquirer*, June 2, 1862.

[75] May 1, 1863 - April 1, 1864, *passim.*

May, 1863 John Randolph Tucker delivered a lecture before the Young Men's Christian Association of Richmond which was subsequently published as a pamphlet. He said the church, though separated, was deeply concerned with having good government and must sustain the state. Civil and religious liberty had been destroyed in the despotic North which had stifled "prayer and religious utterances by the bayonet of its soldiery!" The South was right in the sight of a just God because it waged a war of defense. Tucker held that Southerners were *religiously* bound to defend" the constitution and "obey" the state. "Can the followers of Christ remain at ease in their Zion, when the wildest tornado menaces society . . . ? No war in modern times . . . has been marked by such ferocity—such disregard of private rights—such atrocities toward non-combatants—and such wicked violation of all sanctions of our Holy religion." He asked for prayers and Christian sympathy. "We feel the smile of God's face, and the pleasant shadow of His Almighty wings."[76]

After Gettysburg the Middle District Baptist Association of Virginia "gratefully acknowledge the goodness of God in giving our Confederacy such wise civil and military leaders. . . ."[77] Mr. Renfroe was sickened at the slander and abuse "heaped upon the devoted head of our noble President,"[78] and Moses Hoge lectured widely on the attitude of the outside world toward the Confederacy.[79] The addresses of President Davis to the armies were printed in the *Religious Herald*.[80] Obviously, they were good for civilian morale, too.

Expressions of confidence in and support of the Confederate government were common and outstanding lay and clerical leaders continued until the end of the conflict an aggressive campaign for sustaining the Richmond au-

---

[76] *The Southern Church Justified in Its Support of the South in the Present War* (Richmond, 1863), pp. 23, 27, 34.
[77] *Minutes of the Eightieth Annual Session of the Middle District Baptist Association* . . . (Richmond, 1863), p. 8.
[78] *"The Battle is God's,"* p. 26.
[79] *Op. cit.*, p. 194.
[80] Feb. 18, 1864.

thority. They were a powerful factor in the maintenance of law and order and in the explanation of the necessity for unpopular war measures. The church as a whole compiled an enviable record of unwavering support of and devotion to the Confederate government.

CHAPTER IV

For God and Country

IN THE LONG RUN the fate of the Confederacy would
be determined by the day-to-day activities of Johnny and
Betsy Reb. Their resolution and steadfastness, or lack of it,
would make or break the war effort. Organized propaganda
to mould their views was completely lacking in the middle
years of the nineteenth century, however. In the South
there existed no agency nor any group of leaders as likely
as the church to exercise a direct and guiding influence on
the conduct of the individual citizen. If he looked anywhere
for counsel, it was to the church.

The most impressive way to reach the largest number of
people was by means of a national fast day, either in thanksgiving or humiliation, or both. Recognizing this, President
Davis called for universal observance of the fast nine times
during the life of the Confederacy.[1] Congress, state legislatures, and denominational bodies designated so many more
that a strict compliance with all might have saved enough
food to feed Lee's hungry army.[2] Stephen Elliott thought a
fast day worth a hundred shiploads of arms, "if it be kept

[1] Thursday, June 13, 1861; Friday, Nov. 15, 1861; Friday, May 16,
1862; Thursday, Sept. 18, 1862; Friday, March 27, 1863; Friday, Aug.
21, 1863; Friday, April 8, 1864; Wednesday, Nov. 16, 1864; and
Thursday, March 3, 1865.
[2] John T. Christian, *History of the Baptists in Louisiana* (Nashville,
1923), p. 129; *Minutes of the Fifty-Fifth Anniversary of the Mississippi Baptist Association . . . 1861* (n.p., n.d.), p. 10; Cheshire, *op. cit.*,
pp. 8, 11.

in spirit and in truth,"[3] while a lady from Crawfordsville, Mississippi wrote Governor Pettus in November, 1862: "I think I see behind the cloud a silver beam. From a thorough search of God's word I find no denial of peace to nations that humble themselves before God. Another fast day is absolutely necessary for the good of the land." She suggested three days of self-abnegation, with neither meat nor strong drink, and the "publication" of all violators.[4] Similar requests were received by all Southern governors and comments in the letters and diaries of the period indicate, as General Gorgas noted,[5] that these periods of fasting and prayer were generally observed. In many towns stores were closed and churches were open throughout the day.[6] Inactive armies in the field were accustomed to the suspension of military exercises on such occasions. The *Christian Observer* from Gettysburg to Appomattox took note of much fasting and group prayer, which it was certain would be answered by God.[7] As a matter of fact, it "proved" on June 9, 1864 that fast days on June 13, 1861, May 15, 1862, and March 27 and August 21, 1863 had been followed by Manassas, the Seven Days, Chancellorsville, and Chickamauga.[8] In July, 1861 Congress took note of $5278.58 received by the treasury from donations on the "late fast day" and dedicated its use for soldiers wounded at Manassas.[9]

The *Southern Churchman* recommended that the first week in March, 1862 be spent by all religious congregations

---

[3] *How To Renew Our National Strength*, p. 16.

[4] Mississippi Governor's Records, 1861-1865 (MS, in Mississippi Department of Archives and History, Jackson), series E, file 59.

[5] Vandiver, *op. cit.*, p. 175.

[6] *Christian Observer*, March 10, 1865; Richmond *Sentinel*, May 7, 1864.

[7] Henry Tucker suggested that at one o'clock on each day all citizens of the Confederacy should fall upon their knees to pray for the success of their country (Coulter, *op. cit.*, p. 530).

[8] The belief was expressed by a minister of Vicksburg that the bombardment of the city on September 2, 1862 failed because of the weekly prayer meetings of its citizens (David F. Snipes, "The Churches and Public Opinion in the Confederacy," unpublished thesis, University of Mississippi, 1948, p. 111).

[9] *Acts and Resolutions of the Third Session of the Provisional Congress . . .* (Richmond, 1861), resolution 195.

in prayer,[10] with daily services suitable to the occasion. All subjects which would stir up angry or unkind feelings were to be avoided.

Those who cannot take the field can pray. . . . We are persuaded that the strenuous efforts of the army, accompanied with the most earnest prayers of the entire community—morning, noon, and night—will receive the seal of divine approval in the restoration of an honorable peace.[11]

The ever-present crusade against relatively petty vices, called sins by the evangelical denominations, leads one to suspect that the church was using the war for its own ends. A Baptist Committee on the State of the Country lashed out against worldly-mindedness, relaxation of morals, and self-seeking and decried the "miserable fallacy about the inexorable 'law of trade' with which men strive to quiet their consciences."[12] One religious paper enthusiastically endorsed the declaration of the Richmond *Whig* that, while the nation was imperilled, its people were feasting, frolicking, trafficking and extorting. "We dance and laugh, eat and drink, and are merry, and seem as insensible to the dangers around us as Belshazzar's banqueteers." Dancing and junketing were inhumanly disrespectful and foolish on

[10] The prayer sessions were not always segregated, as witness the prayer of an old Negro before a mixed white and black audience: "Mars Lord, be pleased to blow wid dy bref an' sink de ships of de wicked enemy. Our boys, good marster, will drive 'em from de lan' but thou alone can reach de gunboats" (Bell I. Wiley, *Southern Negroes, 1861-1865*, New Haven, 1938, p. 106).

[11] *Christian Observer*, Feb. 20, 1862. On the eve of Grant's invasion of Virginia the *Religious Herald* suggested that on April 10, 1864 all clergy preach from *Second Chronicles*, 7:13, 14: "If I shut up heaven that there be no rain, or I command the locusts to devour the land, or if I send pestilence among my people; If my people, which are called by my name, shall humble themselves and pray and seek my face, and turn from their wicked ways, then will I hear from heaven and will forgive their sins, and will heal their land" (*Church Intelligencer*, April 8, 1864). Wrote one editor, when all hope seemed gone in 1865: "Beyond all question . . . if we come before the throne of Grace in the spirit of prayer, we shall be heard; the chastening hand . . . shall be turned against our enemies, and His protecting Hand shall cover us" (*Religious Herald*, March 16, 1865).

[12] *Ibid.*, June 4, 1863.

the part of those protected by the living wall of dauntless breasts in the field. The editor called for an end to "kicking up our heels and tripping on the light fantastic toe in the most joyous manner."[13]

Virginia Baptists rebuked the people at home for their public demoralization and relaxation of morals.[14] Archbishop Jean Odin of New Orleans thought that the more evident were God's blessings, the more likely they were "to unfold in us the germs of sinfulness, to excite a hunger and thirst for sensual pleasures and to create an immoderate attachment to the perishable things of this world."[15] The *Christian Observer* cautioned its readers against murmuring and proved with many Biblical quotations that it was a sin.[16] In a pamphlet entitled "Liquor and Lincoln," a physician concluded that the Southern Republic would never achieve independence until its citizens gave up the evil of whiskey drinking. Not only were headstrong soldiers and civilians wrecking the Confederacy (six men in temperance regiments died as contrasted with ten in others), but the Bible conclusively demonstrated they were sending their immortal souls to hell as well.[17] A North Carolinian believed that the war itself had been brought on by sins committed "by the whole people constituting the old United States."[18] And a Virginian asked whether greater success could be expected from the armies "in view of abounding sin and of the moral and spiritual state of the people."[19]

The Reverend Mr. J. M. Hoffmeister enlarged the scope of his attack, crying out against liquor, love of money, licen-

---

[13] *Central Presbyterian*, Jan. 30, 1862.

[14] *Religious Herald*, June 4, 1863.

[15] Blied, *op. cit.*, p. 54.

[16] April 24, 1862.

[17] Physician, *Liquor and Lincoln* (Petersburg, 186-), n.p. Long after the war Benjamin W. Jones believed that God had withdrawn his favor from the South because of "general and shameful" violation of the Sabbath, and intemperance. Except for these "the South might have won her cause" (*Under the Stars and Bars: A History of the Surry Light Artillery*, Richmond, 1909, p. 88).

[18] A. Shotwell to Calvin H. Wiley, March 3, 1864 (in Calvin H. Wiley Papers, North Carolina Department of Archives and History, Raleigh).

[19] *Christian Observer*, Dec. 29, 1864.

tiousness, profanity, desecration of the Sabbath, theft, gambling, murder, lewdness, and whoredoms, all of which he considered Yankee vices.[20]   But it remained for J. L. Burrows to make the supreme effort.   In his fight against the opening of the New Richmond Theatre on February 9, 1863, he declared:

I deem it fitting to give this public notice from the pulpit. . . . a splendid building, with most costly decorations, has been reared from the ashes of the old.   Enough able-bodied men have escaped from conscription . . . in order to accomplish this magnificent work.   A strong corps of actors have been secured, and "twenty *gentlemen*" are these—they can sing and dance; they can mimic fighting while the cars are bringing . . . the dead to their very doors. . . .   They keep themselves out of the war for the noble duty of amusing the populace.   Does it not seem a peculiarly happy time for theatrical amusements?   Shall we all go and laugh and clap to the music while the grasp of relentless foes is tightening upon the throats of our sons . . . ?   What fitter time for opening a theatre in the capital of our bleeding country, unless it could have been on the evening of the battle of Malvern Hill or of Fredericksburg?   Men enough to form an effective artillery company deny themselves the patriotic desire in defending the country against assailing foes [to] devote themselves to your amusement. . . .   The New Richmond Theatre is a public assignation house, where any vile man may be introduced to an infamous woman by paying the price of a ticket.   It is a part of the building especially appropriated to harlots, where your sons may meet them and by their enticements be drawn into the very depths of debasement and vice.[21]

The most challenging sin of all was pointed out by those reformers who thought the war itself a scourge brought on by the Almighty for failure of the South to administer the institution of slavery in conformity with the teachings of

[20] *Come to the Rescue* . . . (Lynchburg, 1863), p. 5.
[21] *The New Richmond Theatre* . . . (Richmond, 1863), pp. 3-4.

the Bible.[22] "Gideon" wrote the Charleston *Courier* that
Southerners could not expect divine assistance until they
repented of and abandoned their sins in connection with
slavery.[23] As Calvin H. Wiley saw the situation,[24] these
sins were (1) overconcern with establishing lawfulness of
slavery according to the Scriptures and neglect of duties
growing out of the master-slave relationship, (2) failure
to insist on sacredness of marriage and parent-child relationship among slaves, (3) disregard of the Sabbath con-
cerning slave labor, (4) dereliction in giving religious
instruction to Negroes, and (5) failure to grant slaves the
protection of the law against hard and cruel masters.[25] As
late as October, 1864 the Georgia Baptist Association
memorialized the state legislature to remedy the "essentially
defective" law which failed to protect the institution of
marriage among slaves.[26] The most fascinating twist to
this movement to humanize slavery was that many people
now spoke out in its favor who had previously remained
silent for fear of encouraging Northern abolitionists. Com-
passionate citizens agreed with R. M. Tydings that, political
relations with the North having been severed, the need for
a united front in the South had disappeared and they might
now "speak of a sin connected with the institution of
slavery."[27] Pressure of greater problems forestalled any
possibility of success for this minor crusade.

[22] Bell I. Wiley, "The Movement to Humanize the Institution of
Slavery during the Confederacy," *Emory University Quarterly*, V,
207-220 (Dec., 1949).

[23] *Ibid.*, V, 216 (Dec., 1949).

[24] In 1864 Wiley received high praise for his *Scriptural Views of
National Trials* (Greensboro, 1863), published in an edition of 2,500
copies. The versatile superintendent of common schools, erstwhile
novelist, editor, and legislator, was told: "You have done an important
service for the country as well as for the church, and it is the very
book for the times." Another correspondent thought the volume
"eminently adapted to the dread ordeal through which we are now
passing" (in Calvin H. Wiley Papers).

[25] Wiley, *op. cit.*, V, 215 (Dec., 1949) ; Bryan, *op. cit.*, XXXIII, 298-
299 (Dec., 1949).

[26] *Minutes of the Baptist Convention of the State of Georgia, 1864*
(Atlanta, 1864), p. 8.

[27] *Florida Sentinel*, March 25, 1862.

With meager understanding of economics, churchmen heaped their most stinging phrases upon that man of greed, the extortioner, who "has churned up an *egregious yearning of the bowels after filthy lucre.*"[28] The *Religious Herald* quoted George Washington on speculators as *"the murderers of our cause,"*[29] and declared they "had heard the voice of the great seducer."[30] One minister feared that these moral sharks and vultures were "devouring the vitals of the Confederate body."[31] In the fall of 1861 the King's Mountain Baptist Association denounced them as "soul-less bipeds, worse enemies than Yankee abolitionists."[32] A year later the *Christian Observer* noted that the pulpit and press had for months been sending forth merited denunciations against exorbitant prices.[33] The Baptists of the Virginia Dover Association bewailed the fact that "the *spirit of gain* seems to have rolled, as a devastating flood, over the land,"[34] and their brothers in Georgia claimed that "Extortioners and the covetous, no more than adulterers and fornicators, idolators, thieves and drunkards, shall inherit the kingdom of God."[35] Bishop Gregg preached in St. David's Church in Austin of the sin of extortion and condemned to hell the sinner.[36] This became an increasingly popular subject of preacher and press as goods became scarce and disastrous inflation menaced the Confederacy.[37]

Judge Thomas S. Gholson of Petersburg urged the government to seize every business in which extortion was practised.[38] When Governor Vance proclaimed a day of fasting,

[28] Stiles, *National Rectitude*, p. 30.
[29] July 18, 1861.
[30] April 16, 1863.
[31] Doggett, *op. cit.*, pp. 7-10.
[32] John R. Logan, *Sketches of the Broad River and King's Mountain Baptist Association* . . . (Shelby, 1887), p. 189.
[33] Dec. 4, 1862.
[34] *Minutes of the . . . Annual Meetings of the Dover Baptist Association* . . . [1862, 1863, 1864, 1865, and 1866] (Richmond, 1866), p. 16.
[35] *Minutes of the Baptist Convention of the State of Georgia, 1862* (Macon, 1862), p. 5.
[36] *Church Intelligencer*, March 15, 1863.
[37] *Christian Observer*, June 9, 1864; Charleston (S. C.) *Mercury*, Aug. 1, 1863; Boyd, *op. cit.*, p. 111.
[38] *Christian Observer*, Dec. 4, 1862.

humiliation, and prayer, the *Church Intelligencer* used it as an occasion to appeal to speculators: "Are we going to present ourselves before the Lord . . . with the secret purpose of still *selling as dear as we can* under some specious pretext? For God's sake . . . let us pause and reflect! Do not let us insult and provoke the Majesty of Heaven and earth by a miserable, blasphemous mocking."[39] The Strong River Baptists in Mississippi warned, "These things should not be so, and it becomes the duty of a Christian to set his face, as a flint, against all such proceedings."[40] In the summer of 1863 Josiah Gorgas wrote in his diary about the sins of Charleston, "full of rottenness." With the fate of Lee's army trembling in the balance at Gettysburg, according to the diarist, a gentleman informed a speculator that a well known officer of the city had been killed. The speculator replied, "You don't say so; what's Calypro this morning?" Calypro was a blockade stock.[41]

Before Christmas of 1863 this "Prayer of the Extortioner" was being circulated in Greensboro, North Carolina:

Our father who art in heaven—I wonder what will be the price of wheat this summer. My crop is fine, very fine. I think I might get at least four dollars for it. I should like to get ten.—Hallowed be thy name—If the season continues I shall make a tremendous crop of corn, and as my cribs are now sufficient to last me two years, it will be a clear profit.—Thy Kingdom come—chickens are a great institution. Before the war I used to sell them for ten cents, now I get two dollars. I can scarcely find it in my heart to pray for peace.—Thy will be done on earth—I believe I won't sell my corn to the soldiers' relief society. They don't give enough—as it is done in heaven. That old steer brought me two hundred dollars. Give us this day our daily bread— my poor neighbor who has a poor husband in the army, and

---

[39] Dec. 10, 1863. Speculators got sharp rebukes as traitors to their country. The *Religious Herald* blasted the enemy, January 29, 1863, in these words: "Yet a little while and that love of money shall pierce the things with many sorrows and drown thy soul in perdition and destruction . . . ."

[40] Bettersworth, *op. cit.*, p. 296.

[41] Vandiver, *op. cit.*, p. 51.

six little children at home, must find it hard to get along. The Lord bless her and hers. Forgive us our trespasses as we forgive those that trespass against us—my old friend Smith was rather hard on me when he said I gouged the poor, but I forgive him—and lead us not into temptation— I am afraid our pastor's prosperity will prove a snare to him. Why, brother Jones sent him a cow and calf—but deliver us from evil. I wish our pastor would quit preaching on extortion. If he don't, I will stop subscription sure. He is really an evil. He won't let a body be at peace—for thine is the kingdom, the power and the glory, forever and ever. I believe I will send some milch cows to market. I hear they are bringing tremendous prices. The merchants do charge awfully for their goods. Lord have mercy on us and save us from extortioners—Amen![42]

Tract No. 3 of the Presbyterian Committee of Publication stated that before the war the South had been free "from this debasing lust of sordidness and love of money. . . . Men have grown rich during the war, the profits of whose business before were barely sufficient for their maintenance." Extortioners, classed with robbers, drunkards, and murderers, "are coining the very blood of the soldier into gold."[43] The discipline of the church was called upon to stop this treason.

The Synod of the Evangelical Lutheran Church issued a terrific blast at speculators in May, 1864. "These men are the active coadjutors of our enemies in enslaving our country, impoverishing our people and ruining our cause." After the war they "must show to an outraged community why they skulked at home . . . when every principle of honor, patriotism and manhood called them . . . to share the perils and sacrifices of the great struggle. . . ."[44]

By 1862 Confederate authorities were showing increasing alarm over the large number of hitherto loyal Southerners who were taking the oath of allegiance to the United

[42] Greensborough (N. C.) *Patriot*, Nov. 5, 1863.
[43] Presbyterian Committee of Publication, *Tract No. 3* (n.p., n.d.), p. 5.
[44] *Minutes of the Second Convention of the General Synod of the Evangelical Lutheran Church* . . . (Savannah, 1864), p. 5.

States.[45]   In Nashville, New Orleans, and Memphis citizens succumbed to overwhelming Union pressure to disavow their Confederate loyalty. The *Christian Observer* proved to the satisfaction of many that such action was wicked, foolish, and useless.[46]   Commenting in May on the state of the country, the Baptists were of the deliberate opinion that no citizen between the lines could take the oath without incurring the guilt of treason or perjury and hoped that no one would "bring so foul a blot on his character."[47]   Later in the year Virginia Presbyterians professed to believe that none of their people had submitted to be oath-bound to the Northern government.[48]

In January, 1863 the Richmond Congress viewed with pride the action of those who had refused to take the oath: " . . . it will be esteemed in the future, a most honorable claim upon the gratitude of their country, and the highest evidence of their duty to truth and principle."[49]   In the same month the commanding general at Vicksburg ordered published in the newspapers a sermon in which the Reverend W. W. Lord roundly denounced the residents of New Orleans who had taken the Federal oath.[50]

The ubiquitous Benjamin M. Palmer, from within the safety of the Confederate lines, circulated a pamphlet on the oath of allegiance in the hope that it was not too late "to rouse those who are involved in this dire calamity . . . to wipe off the dishonor which must else cleave to them forever." He was well aware that a large-scale taking of the oath would sap "the foundations of public morality" and would lead to complete demoralization.   Two classes of

[45] The Diocesan Missionary Society published *Parley the Porter, An Allegory* (Richmond, 186-), by Hannah Moore, "showing how robbers without can never get into a house unless there are traitors within." Although this was obviously a religious tract, it could easily have been applied to the Confederacy itself.

[46] April 17, 1862 .

[47] *Minutes of the Baptist General Association of Virginia, May 30, 1862* (Richmond, 1863).

[48] *Christian Observer*, Oct. 27, 1862.

[49] Palmer's pamphlet on the *Oath of Allegiance* was addressed to John Perkins of Louisiana, who on January 13, 1863 had introduced the resolution in the Confederate Congress.

[50] Bettersworth, *op. cit.*, p. 287.

people had submitted to the oath, those inconsiderable few
who had agreed to secession when they felt it idle to oppose,
and the many who were still secretly loyal to the Confederacy
but had yielded to a pressure without parallel in history.
He made it clear that those who put no faith in the oath
because of the duress involved were still guilty of the sin of
perjury. Calling upon the tempted to render real service
to their country, Palmer advised, "Choose the dungeon and
scaffold a thousand times, rather than transmit the taint
of this leprosy to your offspring."[51] Bishop Wilmer agreed
that all physical evils were as nothing compared with the
shock given public morals by false oaths. With integrity
gone, religion would "dwindle away into hollow cant or
driveling superstition."[52]

An army chaplain by the name of Renfroe, feeling that
after Gettysburg "a spirit of *fear* has gained an influence
over the hearts of many of our fellow citizens," wrote out a
sermon for "the common people." He ridiculed the whining
on the home front, suggesting that most civilians "have
never had to fly to a gunboat, or seek refuge in a mountain,
or hide in a swamp, or run across a river." The army was
steadfast, although at home "there are extortioners, speculators, bloodsuckers, Shylocks, deserters and tories . . .
preying like vultures on the vitals of the country. . . ." The
poor had most at stake in the war as they might lose their
liberty.[53] Another chaplain revealed that soldiers were
"greatly solicitous for the spiritual prosperity of their dear
ones at home"; the army needed no encouragement but was
concerned about reports of gloom and despondency from
behind the lines.[54] Still another assault on lowered civilian
morale came in the Montgomery sermon of Dr. Jackson
Scott who suggested that the great men of history did not
despair: "Patience and perserverance and every proper
and holy effort are necessary. No doubt clouds the future."[55]

[51] *The Oath of Allegiance to the United States Discussed in Its
Moral and Political Bearings* (Richmond, 1863), p. 22.
[52] *Church Intelligencer*, Sept. 28, 1864.
[53] *Op. cit.*, pp. 5, 17.
[54] Letter from A. E. Dickinson, *Religious Herald*, Sept. 17, 1863.
[55] Montgomery (Ala.) *Weekly Mail*, Sept. 2, 1863.

The one personal act with the greatest deadly potential for the fortunes of the Confederacy was desertion. This crime originated more often than not in conditions at home and it was to civilians that the church addressed its attack. The Broad River Baptist Association in the first year of the war advised its Capernaum church to act cautiously with deserters, who "may yet be restored to their country," —but this was not to condone desertion, "a grievous sin" which deserved "the dealings of the church."[56] In 1863 the Holston Conference of Methodists expelled five members for disloyalty, "a crime sufficient to exclude them from the kingdom of grace and glory."[57] Likewise, seventeen slaves were excluded from the Palestine, Mississippi, Baptist Church after they had voluntarily absconded to the Yankees, violating "all the obligations of servants."[58] And one Virginia Baptist church dealt out the same "punishment" to forty-one slaves for escaping to the enemy.[59]

From April, 1862 to January, 1865 the brethren in the Elon, Virginia, Baptist Church were agitated about the conduct of deserters. "The man who is not willing to work for the freedom which God has given us, is a traitor to his country, a hypocrite in the church and unfit to die."[60] In June, 1863 Brother L. B. Anderson declared it had become a rule with most Southern churches to exclude all disaffected persons and deserters. The church resolved that such people were "acting in violation of the laws of God."[61] By August the attention of the congregation was again called to the

[56] Logan, op. cit., p. 100.
[57] William W. Sweet, Methodism in American History (Cincinnati, 1933), p. 288. Dr. E. E. Wiley declared that Southern ministers ought to do more to create public sentiment among their people, unity of thought and purpose and a spirit of loyalty and sacrifices. Bishop John Early was mainly concerned with the support his preachers gave to the Confederacy. See R. N. Price, Holston Methodism (Nashville, 1913), IV, 300, 307-308.
[58] Palestine Baptist Church Record, Sept., 1856 - June, 1936 (MS, in Mississippi College Library, Clinton), Sept. 6, 1863.
[59] Wiley, Southern Negroes, 1861-1865, p. 101.
[60] Minute Book of Elon Baptist Church, Hanover, Virginia, 1861-1865 (MS, in University of Richmond Library), April 5, 1862.
[61] Ibid., June 6, 1863.

subject of disloyal members, and Anderson moved that one W. T. Lane, "now skulking and hiding," be expelled.[62] Action was postponed and several times later "passed over" because no one seemed to know what had happened to Lane. In 1864 the colored members of the church expelled four of their number who had gone over to the enemy, and finally, in January, 1865 Lane was also thrown out.[63]

On February 28, 1864 Chaplain John Paris preached an effective sermon under melancholy circumstances. He had visited each of twenty-two North Carolinians before they were hanged in Kinston for desertion. These men, he warned in a sobering message which was printed and widely circulated, had been good, honest, unoffending citizen-soldiers victimized by mischievous home influences. The real culprits were civilian croakers who had indulged in peace meetings and who had spread their "poisonous contagion of treason" to the army. Skulkers and deserters were usually non-Christians as "Patriotism and Christianity walk hand in hand." Paris called for a revival of that dedication which would set the Confederacy free.[64]

Faith and confidence of the people in their religious leaders assured the acceptance and emulation of a high degree of loyalty and devotion to the Confederacy. At first it was assumed that clergymen were needed at home and they were declared exempt from the provisions of the conscription laws.[65] Preachers could be useful in uplifting "a

[62] *Ibid.*, Aug. 1, 1863.

[63] *Ibid.*, Jan. 14, 1865.

[64] *A Sermon: Preached before Brig. Gen. Hoke's Brigade . . . upon the Death of Twenty-Two Men, Who Had Been Executed in the Presence of the Brigade for the Crime of Treason* (Greensborough, 1864), p. 9.

[65] Albert B. Moore, *Conscription and Conflict in the Confederacy* (New York, 1924), pp. 58-59. Sarah Jones describes in her diary a Baptist country church in Virginia where the ladies of the congregation practiced pistol shooting on the lawn before listening to patriotic speeches and singing patriotic songs. The pastor, Mr. Quence, pronounced himself "ready, not only to *preach* the cause of liberty, but to go himself to join the ranks if need be, as many of his brethren had already done" (*Life in the South from the Commencement of the War, By a British Subject* . . . London, 1863, pp. 283-287).

people who have become terribly possessed with the demon of extortion and other lesser spirits," and thus should remain at their altars to continue their warfare against the Devil, "perhaps the strongest ally of the Yankees."[66] Early in the war Bishop Pierce warned a large crowd of civilians and soldiers at Sparta, Georgia: "Did I know a man here who would refrain to subscribe cotton or money to carry on this war of defense, I would never shake his hand or darken his door with my presence." The bishop was reported to have pledged half his cotton crop.[67]

It is true, however, that those ministers and lay leaders of distinction who went directly into military service set an example of the highest type of Christian patriotism. Warrior-Bishop Polk was only one of many.[68] The president of Hampden-Sidney College was elected captain of a company made up largely of his former students, Professor Dabney of Union Theological Seminary rode with Stonewall Jackson (himself an outstanding Presbyterian layman), one of the secretaries of the American Bible Society returned to North Carolina and a colonelcy in the Confederate Army, Bishop McGill promoted enlistments in the Montgomery Guards, and hundreds of other churchmen doffed their clerical garbs for uniforms.[69] The *Southern Baptist* estimated that half of the Southern clergy was in the service

---

[66] Albert B. Moore, *op. cit.*, p. 59.

[67] *Christian Advocate*, July 4, 1861.

[68] Polk not only directed his troops in the field, but also continued to exert his influence as a Christian priest. He baptised and confirmed Generals Hood, Hardee, and Joseph E. Johnston.

[69] From the North Carolina *Christian Advocate*, May, 1861: "The Reverend Messrs. Atkinson, Presbyterian; Fitzgerald and Smedes, Episcopal; James and Skinner, Baptist; J. W. Tucker, Methodist; and one of the editors of this paper, have attached themselves to the Home Guard, a company organized in this city under the command of Senator Bragg, for the defense of our homes . . . Reverend Willis L. Miller, formerly one of the editors of the *North Carolina Presbyterian*, is Captain of the Thomasville Rifles, which company has offered its services to the state." The Cincinnati (Ohio) *Commercial* was reported as saying that the "Reverends" were the most warlike of the population, breathing out threatenings and slaughter; the language of Christ, "Blessed are the peace makers, for they shall be called the children of God," might be applied to but few clergymen of the country (Nashville [Tenn.] *Republican Banner*, Aug. 11, 1861).

by the spring of 1862.[70]   Many became chaplains, colporteurs, and hospital commissioners and Catholic nuns served
as military nurses.

Testimony regarding the effectiveness of preachers in
uniform and as chaplains indicates they were a mixed lot,[71]
but even those who failed in their new duties may have been
an inspiration to the people back home. As the *Daily Mississippian* put it, the warrior preachers had time to fight
the devil after flogging the Yankees.[72]   There were, of
course, many stories of fighting Confederate chaplains. One
concerned a Virginian who had taken command in battle,
after the officers had been killed. He ordered his men to
hold their fire until the enemy closed in, and then, his face
aglow with excitement, he blurted out: "May God have
mercy on their souls; give 'em hell, boys! give 'em hell."[73]

In areas conquered by Union forces, ministers such as
Leacock, Goodrich, and Hall of New Orleans, and Marshall,
Lord, and Rutherford of Vicksburg, refused to take the oath
of allegiance and were banished into the Confederacy where
they became particularly strong morale boosters because of
their example. Benjamin Palmer ranged up and down the
country during the whole of the war, assuming the appear-
ance of a prophet of the Lord. A general in Mississippi
declared Palmer to be worth a thousand soldiers to the cause.
As Sherman marched through Georgia the great orator was
believed to have strengthened the hearts and hands of many
people.[74] He apparently never wearied of striking for country, home, "for the altars of our worship, the graves of our

[70] *Daily Nashville* (Tenn.) *Union*, May 6, 1862.

[71] Bell I. Wiley " 'Holy Joes' of the Sixties: A Study of Civil War
Chaplains," *Huntington Library Quarterly*, XVI, 287-304 (May,
1953).

[72] (Jackson), April 10, 1863.

[73] Theodore Gerish and John Hutchinson, *The Blue and the Gray*
(Bangor, 1884), p. 65. One preacher is supposed to have presented a
revolver to a soldier before his departure to the war, with the following injunction: "If you get into a tight place and have to use it, ask
God's blessing if you have time, but be sure and not let the enemy
get the start of you. You can say amen after you shoot" (Memphis
Daily Appeal, Jan. 2, 1862).

[74] DesChamps, *op. cit.*, XIX, 21 (Sept., 1953).

dead," and for the prerogatives of God and His Kingly supremacy over the earth.

Perhaps the most influential example of all was set by those ministers who remained within union lines but declined to swear Federal allegiance. Such patriots were arrested on a wholesale scale in Nashville,[75] and South Carolina Baptists resolved in July, 1862 that "We look with admiration on their constancy and fortitude."[76] Catholic leaders in New Orleans were particularly difficult for General Butler to win over even to neutrality.[77] As late as March, 1864 Father John Finacune almost embroiled two young priests and caused "great scandal" in Lebanon, Kentucky by toasting Jefferson Davis.[78]

A major cause of desertion on the part of otherwise patriotic soldiers was the consuming fear that their loved ones at home were in danger of exposure or starvation. Hence, it was a matter of morale as well as of Christian charity that soldiers' indigent families be provided for. State legislatures allocated millions of dollars for relief of civilians in distress but these programs broke down more and more on the local level and the churches took over. Complicating the confusion as the war continued to take its heavy toll was the fact that, as expressed starkly by the Virginia Presbyterians, " . . . our widows and orphans are multiplying."[79]

Within a week of the fall of Fort Sumter the *Central Presbyterian* took notice of relief work being performed by women of the churches,[80] and by the Fourth of July the *Christian Advocate* was singing the praises of the Georgia program for the support of the families of volunteers, financed by public and private donations.[81] Religious papers

[75] Sweet, *Methodism in American History*, p. 288.
[76] *Minutes of the Forty-Second Anniversary of the State Convention of the Baptist Denomination in S. C.* (Columbia, 1862), p. 144.
[77] Roger Baudier, *The Catholic Church in Louisiana* (New Orleans, 1939), p. 427.
[78] Blied, *op. cit.*, p. 39.
[79] *Minutes of the Synod of Virginia, at Their Session in Salem* . . . (Richmond, 1863), p. 332.
[80] April 20, 1861.
[81] July 4, 1861.

continued to be deeply concerned with this colossal problem which they publicized at every opportunity, as when the *Christian Observer* noticed with evident satisfaction the disbursal of supplies to 1,838 soldiers' families in a single day in New Orleans.[82] The same paper in 1864 with obvious intent called to the attention of wealthy farmers the example of the Twelfth Mississippi Regiment and Archie's Tennessee Brigade which had offered one day's ration a week for relief of the poor.[83]

The North Carolina Presbyterian Synod set up committees to raise and spend money to provide for the education of children of deceased and disabled veterans.[84] In Alabama the Tuskeegee Baptist Association, asserting that "the danger from the rear is greater than the danger in front," renewed its efforts to eliminate poverty in soldiers' families.[85] Dover Baptists collected $2200 at one meeting for education of the children of those in the army,[86] and Georgia Baptists raised $200,000 and proposed to scrape together two million more for a home for war orphans.[87] The Alabama Baptists were praised for similar action by the *Religious Herald*,[88] which waged a continuous campaign on the necessity to provide for the education of orphaned children.[89] When Moses Hoge returned from England in October, 1863 with a shipload of Bibles, he was requested "in an almost official form" to lecture on the experiences of his mission and in so doing he raised several thousand dollars for the relief of soldiers' families.[90]

These are only scattered examples of the efforts of religious leaders to maintain a high level of morale throughout endless weary weeks of day-to-day living. In effect, they held society together, kept the schools and churches running,

[82] Feb. 2, 1862.
[83] June 9, 1864.
[84] *Minutes of the Forty-Nineth* [sic] *Sessions . . .* , p. 23.
[85] Bessie Martin, *Desertion of Alabama Troops from the Confederate Army: A Study in Sectionalism* (New York, 1932), p. 145.
[86] *Minutes of the Dover Baptist Association . . .* , Sept. 14, 1864.
[87] *Religious Herald*, April 27, 1864.
[88] Nov. 26, 1863.
[89] Aug. 8, 11, 1864.
[90] *Op. cit.*, p. 194.

led the cheers in time of victory, and consoled those in sorrow. The *Central Presbyterian* surmised in the fall of 1861 that the South would develop many patriots of the type of Abigail Adams and that they would show the world "that we are a people never to be conquered."[91]   At least the first part of its prophecy proved accurate, for women were in the forefront of many of the activities carried on by local churches.[92]   For the duration of the war the religious press was quick to commend any meritorious action which might further the war effort—for example, when manufacturers put aside portions of their production for outright relief or for sale to the poor at cost.[93]   Much of the credit for keeping those individuals steadfast who stood by the Confederacy until every hope was gone must be given to the church.

[91] Oct. 5, 1861.

[92] Stephen Elliott praised the spirit of Southern women: " . . . the attitude of woman is sublime. She bears it all and says: He died for the cause. He perished for his country. I would not have it otherwise, but I should have liked to have given the dying boy my blessing, the expiring husband my last kiss of affection, the bleeding lover the comfort of knowing that I kneeled beside him" (*Sermon Preached in Christ's Church, Savannah, September 18, 1862*), p. 17.   According to the *Christian Observer*, March 6, 1862, "The times through which we are passing will never be rightly illustrated without a thorough appreciation of the share which the mothers and daughters have in them."

[93] *Christian Observer*, May 5, 1864.

CHAPTER V

The Threat of Yankeeism

THE SOUTH never again approached the delirious enthusiasm of the days after Fort Sumter, although it did experience several periods of steady confidence and even exultation.[1] As these faded into times of gloom and despondency, the people, increasingly paralyzed by war weariness, might yet be stirred up to desperate resistance, if convinced of the terrible alternatives to victory. To achieve this purpose, the church stepped up its campaign of fear and hate, playing on the baser passions with a fierce determination to outlast the North regardless of cost.

Although Daniel I. Dreher spoke of "plunder, arson, murder, and rape" as early as June, 1861[2] and Bishop McGill mentioned 30,000 handcuffs the Union army was supposed to have brought to Manassas,[3] the type of "atrocity" usually mentioned in that year was later shrugged off as one of the natural consequences of war.[4] Civilians became hardened to deeds which in peace-time would have been considered barbarous, and so it became necessary to

[1] The title of this chapter was suggested by the following statement in the Tuskeegee (Ala.) *South Western Baptist*: "This war will give to the pages of history another word, expressive of a still deeper dye of depravity than Europe ever dreamed of. It is Yankeeism." See Coulter, *op. cit.*, pp. 81-82.

[2] *Op. cit.*, p. 13.

[3] Blied, *op. cit.*, p. 61.

[4] T. V. Moore spoke of the threat of men killed, women "dishonored before our eyes," homes pillaged, and fields laid waste in his *Discourse before the Congregations of the First and Second Presbyterian Churches, Richmond, November 15, 1861* (Richmond, 1861), p. 21.

increase the shrillness of the shouting with each passing year. At first, then, the propaganda technique seemed to require ridicule of the Yankee rather than to stamp him with the seal of brutality.

The situation in the spring of 1862, however, loomed more desperate than at any time until the fall of Atlanta. The *Christian Observer*, having accepted the certainty of a long war, screamed that *"Defeat will be death to us,* and worse than death, it *will be* INFAMY. We and our children will be slaves to the North, and entail the curse of servitude under a military despotism for ages to come." Editor Amasa Converse disclaimed any notion of creating panic but he insisted that his readers see the crisis. "To meet it, let our country become a wide camp, with a million men in arms, resolved by the help of God to drive the enemy from our borders."[5]

The *Central Presbyterian* likewise was sure the North would not crumble, for she must conquer the South to recover the huge debts she was piling up. Union leaders proposed "a gigantic scheme for colonization, prosecuted in behalf of a needy, degraded and lawless population, which can neither be fed nor tolerated at home. . . . Our people will be driven from their homes and lands [to be taken over] by the refuse of the rural districts, and offscouring of Northern and European cities."[6] The *Southern Christian Advocate* added that "we all shall become miserable slaves and paupers, crushed under the heel of a tyrannical mob. . . . To lose our cause is to lose everything except our souls, and to many this loss also would be imminent." The wealth of the South was to be absorbed to pay for its subjugation.[7] During McClellan's advance on Richmond, Dr. Thornwell, six weeks before his death, went somewhat further when he declared in a pamphlet that the Confederacy must become fully alive to the magnitude of the emergency. All private interests must be sacrificed and

---

[5] March 6, 1862.
[6] April 10, 1862.
[7] Quoted in *Christian Observer*, May 8, 1862.

the spirit of faction must go, as defeat would bring homes pillaged, cities sacked, men hanged, and women "the prey of brutal lust." The slave would pass away as had the Indian and within the Confederacy there would be re-enacted the history of Poland and Hungary.[8] As the president of Emory College saw it, with the defeat of the South would go the last hope of freedom, the last home of a pure Gospel, and the phrase "colonial vassalage" would hardly convey the faintest notion of the real condition of the country.[9]

George Fitzhugh believed that panic would pass away in a few days. In any case, Southerners should arouse from their despondency and inaction, should encourage each other with words and example and should quit useless repinings. After all, the North had taken only a few seaports and Nashville, which might have been expected. But Fitzhugh also spoke in terms of alternatives. If not ready to repel attack, the South must look forward to loss of slaves and other property and to a miserable existence, dragged out in disgrace, poverty, and slavery.[10]

Within a year the mild-mannered educational and religious leader in North Carolina, Calvin H. Wiley, declared in a printed document that the North had "summoned to its aid every fierce and cruel and licentious passion of the human heart," and had called for battle "by the assassin's dagger, the midnight torch, by poison, famine and pestilence." The Federal government would place under the ban of civilization and Christianity the people on whom it was making war, as a race whose extermination would be

[8] *Central Presbyterian*, May 15, 1862.

[9] Bryan, *op. cit.*, XXXIII, 285 (Dec., 1949).

[10] Quoted from *DeBow's Review* by the *Christian Observer*, March 6, 1862. Joseph Cross helped to perpetuate a story that Abraham Lincoln was part Negro, that his mother was of "low association," and that from his father he had received cruel treatment. "This had the effect of hardening a nature by no means soft, and rendering him a fit tool for carrying out the hellish purposes of the Abolition party . . . . The bastard son of Hannah Hanks has a grudge against the human family" (*op. cit.*, II, 19-21).

a deliverance to the world, he added.[11]

With relatively free exchange of newspapers and periodicals between the sections, it was both natural and effective for Rebel propagandists to turn to their advantage the words of Yankee extremists. The *Central Presbyterian* had expected the secular press of the North to be "perfectly fiendish," but apparently was surprised to find religious papers following the same course.[12] Their type was "dipped in blood" in presenting the world with the darkest chapter ever written in the history of human depravity.[13] According to one religious editor, who had been encouraged by "an estimable lady" to print something encouraging, *Harper's Weekly* was carrying stories about experiments with Union sentiment in Baltimore, Nashville, and New Orleans. If not successful, "the bulk of the WHITE PEOPLE IN THE SOUTH WILL HAVE TO BE EXILED." Davis and Beauregard would "expiate their crimes on the rack or at the stake." *Harper's* also claimed that Rebels had shot into ambulances, poisoned wells, and planted torpedoes. "They cut off the heads of our dead at Manassas; they boiled the

---

[11] *Circular to the Authorities and People of North Carolina* (Greensboro, 1863), p. 8. On December 24, 1863 The *Christian Observer* published, with obvious relish, an article from the Richmond *Whig* on Lincoln's 10 per cent amnesty plan: "The very liberal terms on which Lincoln proposes to take us back into the Yankee Union are set forth in the Proclamation. We have only to confess that we are felons, needing to be pardoned—that we are cowards, unwilling long to fight for liberty and rights—that we are fools having undertaken an enterprise of which we were incapable—to kiss the hand dripping with blood of our kinsmen—to perjure our souls by swearing assent to the measures of a usurper, and allegiance to a Government that we abhor—to fix upon the memory of our glorious dead the everlasting strain of having fallen in a guilty cause—to yield up the noble leaders we have chosen to the executioner—to discharge from bondage our slaves, uprooting our whole social and industrial system, and overrunning the land with hordes of ignorant, lawless, corrupted and dangerous negroes—to become members of a government perverted, revolutionized and running into a despotism—to yield up all our interests to the legislature of a Congress besotted with fanaticism and rancorously inimical—to acknowledge that the Yankee is the superior race—to stand before the world disgraced, and to be mocked and jeered and spit upon by our conquerors—to be the laughing stock of the satirist and the butt of the historian—and to doom our children to shame and bondage."

[12] May 11, 1861.

[13] May 18, 1861.

bodies to get the bones more readily; they buried our brave brothers with their faces down; they swung their heads as trophies upon their homeward march . . . they bayoneted the wounded in the Virginia valley; they blew their heads off with muzzles held close. . . ."[14] Northern church journals were quoted as having recommended the blotting out of South Carolina, and the elimination of Florida, "not as a beloved sister, but as an abortion."[15] It was suggested, too, that the Reverend Doctor Stanton had paid his respects to his fellow Presbyterians, Thornwell and Palmer: "I expect to meet some of these men in heaven; but before that, I expect to see them hanged on earth; AND I SHALL REJOICE IN THAT HANGING."[16]

The Reverend J. W. Jackson was reported to have thundered from his Philadelphia pulpit that the United States should "carry the war to the knife, to the hilt, and to the death of every rebel."[17] Dr. Kirk in the Boston *Christian Banner* had proclaimed his love for Southern men; that is, until they had undertaken to destroy the best government on earth and to turn the country into a slave pen. "Then," he added, "we lay aside our aversion to blood, and go, like Abraham at God's command, the naked knife in hand, to make the bloody offering as priests of the Most High. . . ." Incensed by Kirk's claim that the South had won eight victories to fifty-six for the North, the *Religious Herald* denounced him as a liar.[18]

In a short-lived little publication "devoted exclusively to the soldier," the *Biographical Pen*, Josiah Davis wrote a scornful essay on Henry Ward Beecher's antics in his Plymouth Church pulpit. Speaking on the Emancipation Proclamation, Beecher had derided the Constitution as mere sheepskin parchment and had declared the North was suffering for having winked so long at slavery for the sake of

[14] *Christian Observer*, July 17, 1862.
[15] *Ibid.*, Nov. 20, 1862.
[16] Quoted from the *True Presbyterian* by *Christian Observer*, Oct. 16, 1862.
[17] *Ibid.*, Aug. 12, 1862.
[18] July 31, 1862.

commerce. As the war had already cost two billion dollars, Beecher was of the opinion that the Lord, the great Tax-Collector, would get back pretty much every penny that the North had made out of slavery. As a matter of fact, God was having a gay time collecting his due. Editor Davis was shocked that Beecher's audience had laughed at such horrible blasphemy.[19]

A sure-fire method of creating a feeling of disgust for the Yankees appeared in the *Religious Herald*. Union officers, it stated with considerable loathing, had been seen in captured cities parading up and down the streets with Negro women on their arms. They would kiss colored babies "for the sake of abducting their mothers." Negro women, of course, were highly flattered, and when waiting on Yankee officers, "would lean over their shoulders, cheeks close, arms fondly extended around their necks toward the cups—and with an air of complacent condescension, say, 'Do let me fill your cup, sir.' "[20] A similar approach was tried by the same paper when it quoted from the Boston *Freedman*, a periodical apparently published for the benefit of slaves in the South. According to the story: " 'John, do you love God?' asked the teacher of a bright little boy of six. 'O yes, Missus, I love God a heap.' 'What makes you love him?' 'Mammy says He gives me breath every day, and *He helped us to run off from old Massa*.' "[21]

The triple-edged combination of horrors at the North, atrocities of Northerners in the South, and the threat of overwhelming barbarism if the Confederacy failed, moved into high gear in the last two years of the war. Stories of desecrated churches, desolated homes, and outraged women became common. Ladies in occupied Natchez, before they could worship God, were insulted "at the hands of a dirty, thieving set of rapscallions hardly fit to have their heads blown off and used for fertilizer for the next cotton crop."[22] Bishop Andrew wrote to the *Christian Advocate* of the refu-

[19] (Lynchburg, Va.), Oct. 22, 1862.
[20] July 10, 1862.
[21] August 4, 1864.
[22] Augusta *Daily Chronicle and Sentinel*, Sept. 15, 1863.

gees passing through Alabama on their way to Georgia. He suggested this as one of the darkest chapter in the history of savage warfare and was sure its purpose was to destroy the Southern white population. Negroes were encouraged to murder whites and colored women and children had died by the thousands in pens and camps.[23]

The most gruesome report on a Northern preacher came earlier in the war. It was alleged that a Reverend Mr. Black had conducted a religious service in Newport, Kentucky in rather flambuoyant fashion. The church was ornamented with United States flags and brass eagles, and the hymns for the day were the "Star Spangled Banner," "The Red, White and Blue," and "Hail Columbia." In his prayer the preacher had called on the Lord to preserve the Union "even though blood may come out of the wine-press, even unto the horses' bridles, by a space of a thousand and six hundred furlongs." Thus warmed up, Mr. Black got down to cases in his sermon:

I trust our troops will rally and wipe out the disgrace of Manassas, though it cost the life of ever rebel under arms. Let Davis and Beauregard be captured, to meet the fate of Haman. Hang them up on Mason's and Dixon's line, that traitors may be warned. Let them hang until vultures shall eat their rotten flesh from their bones; let them hang until the crows shall build their filthy nests in their skeletons; let them hang until the rope rots, and let their dismembered bones fall so deep into the earth that God Almighty can't find them in the day of resurrection.[24]

Yankee atrocities became progressively more brutal, according to a Senate committee reporting in July, 1863 on events in Arkansas, Alabama, and the Carolinas. A catalogue of property stolen was enough "to make an angel weep, a devil blush, and anything but a Yankee relent." It would shock the feelings of a Sepoy and crimson the cheek of a Comanche. The war was not merely savage; "it is

[23] *Ibid.*, Nov. 20, 1863.
[24] William W. Sweet, *The Methodist Episcopal Church and the Civil War* (Cincinnati, 1912), pp. 56-57.

unmixed and unmitigated Yankee." Northerners had far
outdone their Puritan ancestors who had burned witches,
hanged Quakers, and cured heresy by cropping ears and
splitting noses. At Mrs. Bell's plantation in Louisiana,
Yankees fleeing Vicksburg had treated the more handsome
Negro women "à la Yankee Doodle," and in Baltimore, Miss
Carey, "a high-toned lady, as pure as an icicle," had been
arraigned for displaying the Confederate flag.[25] LeRoy Lee
pointed out that the North undoubtedly had a pre-deter-
mined purpose to exterminate white Southerners, which
logically left them no recourse except "fierce, bloody, protracted war."[26] One Confederate editor claimed that a
northwestern Methodist conference had endorsed "Emancipation, Confiscation, Conflagration, and Extermination."[27]

Atrocity-wise editors of the secular press were not slow
in pointing out that cold-blooded Union soldiers "drunken
with wine, blood, and fury" were allowed to enter "every
dwelling at their pleasure, plunder the property, ravish the
women, burn the house, and proceed to the next."[28] Stated
the Augusta *Register*, "We are informed that the incarnate
devils ravished some of the nicest ladies of the town" of
Milledgeville.[29] Religious editors seem to have been milder

[25] Cross, *op. cit.*, III, *passim*. Five chapters are devoted to atrocities.
[26] From East Tennessee came the report of the Reverend George
Eagleton, telling of a severe whipping he had received at the hands
of Northern soldiers for preaching at New Market. The *Religious
Herald*, Sept. 1, 1864, called this "the most diabolical and savage act
of maliknant cruelty of which we have record."
[27] *Church Intelligencer*, Dec. 4, 1863.
[28] Richmond *Examiner*, March 7, 1864. The Montgomery *Weekly
Mail*, Jan. 14, 1864, argued that the horrors of peace without victory
would be worse than those of war, the Yankees being "a mean mob
of the lowest of the white races of the earth." The Charleston *Mercury*, Jan. 12, 1864, saw the meaning of subjugation: "Then will
come the time to garrison every town with Yankee guards; to garrison
every court with Yankee judges; every church with Yankee preachers
. . . We must sink at once to a vassal people, object of scorn, at best
the pity of the whole world." From the April 18, 1864 Richmond
Examiner, "The white wives, which they [the North] have promised
to their negro followers, are our sisters and our sweethearts. Think
of that, men of the South, and strike harder the next time you meet
the foe. Unless you drive these wretches howling back to their haunts
of impurity and keep them there, you will be 'of all men most
miserable.' "
[29] Dec. 2, 1864.

in their claims of outrage against Southern women. For instance, five young ladies were banished from Vicksburg because they walked out of the Episcopal Church where the prayer was being read for President Lincoln.[30] A "brutal outrage" occurred when Union soldiers presented a pistol to the head of "Mrs. D," who somehow managed to run from the house to save her life. A certain young lady was chased around the room a few times but she, too, effected her escape.[31] When Columbia was pillaged, in isolated cases the dresses of the ladies "were torn from their bodies by villains who expected to find jewels or plate concealed."[32] Church editors were apparently more squeamish about rape charges than their secular brothers although the Virginia Baptists did suggest that unprotected women had been subjected to imprisonment, "and various sufferings and indignities, worse than death itself. . . ."[33]

From the beginning to end, Southern churchmen rang the changes on the impending collapse of the North, with all kinds of substantiating evidence.[34] The Lincoln government was enforcing its decrees by a reign of violence,[35] financial distress was driving a large part of the population to choosing between enlistment in the army and starvation,[36] and military censorship had already developed "an organized system of lying" in the press,[37] an instrument "of gigantic power to create, to form, to control, energize and direct public sentiment."[38] A New York *Times* reporter wrote that General Longstreet had been killed at Fredericks-

[30] *Christian Observer*, Jan. 28, 1864.
[31] *Ibid.*, April 7, 1864.
[32] *Ibid.*, March 16, 1865.
[33] *Minutes of the Baptist General Association of Virginia* (Richmond, 1864), June 3, 1864.
[34] *Christian Observer*, June 9, 1864.
[35] *Proceedings of the Southern Baptist Convention*, p. 63.
[36] *Christian Observer*, Feb. 20, 1862. According to one preacher the North was bankrupt, was kept subdued by a "vile tyranny," and had suffered a million casualties. Conscription was enforced by the bayonet and there was "dissension and dis-affection in [Lincoln's] counsels." See I. R. Finley, *The Lord Reigneth* (Richmond, 1863), p. 13.
[37] *Christian Observer*, July 24, 1862.
[38] *Ibid.*, July 23, 1863.

burg and that Lee, severely wounded, was in full retreat.[39]
Altogether, infidelity, blasphemy, intemperance, and licentiousness were stalking the land and it would seem that a
righteous God had abandoned the Yankees.[40] Grant butchered tens of thousands of young men needlessly, declared
one editor:

What to him that his heaps of slaughtered victims should
lie unburied save by such sepulture as dogs and hogs and
buzzards can afford to putrifying corpses! What that the
midnight air should be rent with the groans and agonizing
screams of thousands of his wounded braves for days together, as they perished by slow torture! What that the
world would weep, if he may become a president.[41]

He could hardly have known that Grant was destined to
secure the presidency, but after he had declared, "Let us
have peace." Sherman received even shorter shrift for
"personal violence and outrages that make the blood boil . . .
and steel the heart in its fierce determination never again
to live in union with a people who are guilty of such inhuman
and diabolical deeds."[42] The North avowed: "Rebels have
no rights. Their lives are forfeit. If we slay them all, we
only do justice."[43] And so the South was told that its only
choice was between victory and extermination.

In both pulpit and religious press there was exaggeration
and falsification of conditions abroad and in the North,[44]

[39] *Ibid.*, June 16, 1864.
[40] *Church Intelligencer*, Feb. 19, 1864.
[41] *Christian Observer*, June 23, 1864. For a longer and even more
bitter account of "the situation" see Cross, *op. cit.*, II, 7-8.
[42] *Religious Herald*, Dec. 23, 1864.
[43] *Church Intelligencer*, Jan. 26, 1865.
[44] *Central Presbyterian*, April 10, 1862. An example of prejudiced
writing may be found in an article on "The Landing of the Pilgrims,"
featured in the religious *Child's Index*, Sept., 1864. From the Pilgrims
had descended "the Yankee nation, which is now trying to deprive us
not only of our religious liberty, but of every kind of liberty. They
refuse to let us have Bibles . . . They drag our preachers from our
pulpits, and send them to prison. They deprive us of our churches,
and burn them or use them as stables wherever they have taken . . .
our towns, and if they conquer us they will take away all our churches
. . . and not even let us pray in our families as we wish . . . They
are blinded by fanaticism and infidelity" (quoted in Bryan, *op. cit.*,
XXXIII, 295-296, Dec. 1949).

but such distortion as occurred in news of the Confederacy seems to have been due mainly to faulty communication and undue optimism rather than to deliberate lying. The *Christian Observer* of July 16, 1863, for instance, admitted that its last issue had given an exaggerated account of Lee's success at Gettysburg. Its excuse was that "glorious news continued to come in up to the hour of going to press," but this apology hardly presaged objective reporting of the Pennsylvania campaign. On August 6 the same paper claimed the Union had paid "a thousand-fold more in life and treasure" than Vicksburg was worth and considered its capture a white elephant for the North. In August, 1863 Lee was watching the enemy in Virginia, Bragg in Tennessee, and "Johnston, in Mississippi, [was] ready to pounce on Grant, should he make any unguarded move from . . . Vicksburg."[45] Later the Southern victory at Chickamauga had "defeated the great scheme for our subjugation; the ambitious hopes of its authors are in the dust." A casual reader of this church paper might have assumed that the whole South was on the verge of redemption "from the despotic tread of the Yankee invader."[46] And so, perhaps, the editors in mid-1864 sincerely believed.

[45] *Church Intelligencer*, Aug. 14, 1863.
[46] *Christian Observer*, Oct. 1, 1863; May 26, 1864.

CHAPTER VI

Not Even Bayonets Have Done More

THE CHURCH was the most powerful organization influencing the lives of men and women in the South in the days before and during the Confederacy. Clergymen led the way to secession. They were quite successful in helping the people to identify God, the right, and the destiny of history with slavery, the Confederacy, and the war. They established the certainty that the Lord was with his chosen people in victory and defeat. They were responsible for the association of religion with politics and war. They unwaveringly supported the administration of Jefferson Davis. By personal example and by supplication they exerted a tremendous pressure on individual conduct. And when war weariness caused the people to hesitate and falter, the men of God boldly attempted to sustain and strengthen civilian tenacity by a resort to the use of atrocity stories and fear techniques.

In spite of periodic clamor for unanimity in thought and deed, it was never achieved among the peoples of the many-regioned South. Southern religious leadership was not universally anxious to destroy the Union. Quakers refused to support the war, numerous preachers in the occupied territory became lukewarm in their zeal or went over to the enemy, and some churchmen, not only in East Tennessee and Western Virginia but also in the Gulf States, remained loyal to the United States throughout the conflict. Border-state clergy reflected the uncertainty of the civilian population. And there can be no doubt that religious leaders of all denominations gave the Confederacy their overwhelming support and that as a group they were undoubtedly the most powerful factor in the maintenance of a high degree of morale among the people of the South.[1]

Obviously the campaign of the church failed. The odds against success may have been so great' that only the intervention of a jealous God could have brought the Confederacy to triumph. As many writers in recent years have demonstrated, the people of the new nation lost their will to fight. Whether it would have been otherwise, if formulators of public opinion, such as politicians and editors of secular papers, had been as effective as the churchmen, must remain one of the uncertainties of history.

Much Confederate religious propaganda must have backfired. Sermons and editorials often had a dual purpose. For example, the major goal of thousands of tracts was the acceptance of Christ by the reader who might also be argued out of bad habits, such as drinking and swearing. These miniature sermons contained stories of Christian lives gathered from the Bible and the roll of honor of Confederate heroes. Many emphasized home. It seems reasonable, then, that "The Sentinel," a tract written by a Presbyterian lady at a military post and published in the interest of salvation but extolling patriotism, might have suggested desertion as an alternative to regeneration.[2] The Richmond *Examiner* claimed that colporteurs who circulated on the

---

[1] The Augusta *Register* claimed, Nov. 4, 1864, that newspapers had done more for the success of the Confederacy than any other civilian element. "They have . . . aroused patriotism of the people to every demand made upon them . . . They have educated the minds of the people to every great and important change in the policy of our Government." On the other hand, it may be argued that the press had been responsible, as indeed were the preachers, for a great deal of over-confidence. For example, the *Central Presbyterian*, May 1, 1862, calld the fall of New Orleans an "unexpected calamity," which it certainly was, due in large part to the newspapers of New Orleans themselves. In like measure, the people had been taught that Vicksburg was impregnable and they were thoroughly shocked when it capitulated. See Cross, *op. cit.*, III, 72.

[2] The author bluntly suggested to soldiers that "your business is to die . . . you must face the *cannon's* mouth, and stand before a volley of fire . . . "

eve of expected battles little pamphlets headed, "Are You Ready to Die?" and "Sinner, You Are Soon to be Damned!" were doing more harm than good.[3] Ministers unquestionably gave conflicting advice—some encouraged a scorched-earth policy while others ridiculed it.[4] However simple the message, some citizens were sure to misinterpret it, as the Mississippi women who celebrated a day of fasting and humiliation with a church fair and supper.[5] Political sermons involving personalities and differences of opinion on secular matters were bound to becloud the most urgent objective, support of the war.

With such shortcomings in mind, it still must be admitted that the Southern clergy in identifying church and state gave powerful support to their holy cause.

Of the overwhelming influence of the clergy on the people of the Confederacy, there is almost limitless testimony in the diaries and letters of the period. A Baton Rouge minister who tried to stem the tide of secession in Louisiana confided that his congregation had been won over by Palmer's Thanksgiving sermon.[6] Writing on the state of feeling in Texas, W. A. Fletcher reported that "the impression I received through public clamor dethroned what little reason I had, as I believed the most the politician said, and all the preacher said, because he proved it by the Bible. . . ."[7] On President Davis's first fast day, a partially literate overseer recorded his praper that:

Every Black Republican in the hole combined whorl . . . that is opposed to negro slavery . . . shall be trubled with pestilents and calamitys . . . and O God I pray the to Direct a bullet or a bayonet to pirce the Hart of every northern soldier theet invades southern soill and after the Body has

[3] Quoted in *Florida Sentinel*, March 4, 1862.
[4] Augusta *Chronicle and Sentinel*, March 13, 1863; *Central Presbyterian*, March 13, 1862; *Christian Observer*, Dec. 4, 1862.
[5] Bettersworth, *op. cit.*, p. 294.
[6] From an unpublished diary of Thaddeus McRae, quoted in DesChamps, *op. cit.*, XIX, 16 (Sept., 1953).
[7] *Rebel Private, Front and Rear* (Beaumont, 1908), p. 7.

rendered up its traterist sole give it a trators reward a birth in the Lake of Fires and Brimstone. . . .[8]

In his message to the South Carolina legislature in November, 1862 Governor Pickens spoke of the unanimity and deep enthusiasm of the whole people arising "from the fervor and religious zeal in our cause which our clergy and laity, of all denominations, have manifested. They have made it a holy war."[9] An enthusiastic writer, who had listened to Stephen Elliott in March, 1863, declared that those who had heard his eloquent and encouraging appeal would testify that "his trumpet has given no uncertain tone. Oh! that every soldier . . . could have heard him. It would have nerved their hearts anew for the struggle. It would have made the veriest coward a hero panting to do or die."[10] And William Porcher Miles, chairman of the military committee in the Confederate House of Representatives, testified as late as February, 1865 that "The clergy have done more for the success of our cause, than any other class. They have kept up the spirits of our people, have led in every philanthropic movement. . . . Not even the bayonets have done more."[11]

It may be more to the point to examine the testimony of leading Unionists. Practically every statement of the quotable Parson Brownlow condemned Southern preachers for inaugurating and carrying on the war. He indicted Baptist, Episcopalian, Methodist, and Presbyterian ministers, not only as traitors but also as individuals whose private conduct would bear investigation. It was his claim that a Knoxville Presbyterian had got up a union prayer meeting

[8] Quoted in E. Merton Coulter (ed.), Ulrich B. Phillips, *The Course of the South to Secession* (New York, 1939), p. 143.

[9] *Reports and Resolutions of the General Assembly . . . 1862* (Columbia, 1862), p. 19.

[10] *Church Intelligencer*, March 28, 1863. As the result of a "beautiful and impressive effort of Christian eloquence, imbued with the holy emotions of a lofty patriotism," on the part of Bishop McGill, according to the Richmond *Dispatch*, "The soldier's bosom was seen to heave with mingled emotions of patriotism and indignation" (Blied, *op. cit.*, p. 61).

[11] *Christian Observer*, Feb. 23, 1865.

to beseech the Lord to sink Burnside's fleet and raise Lincoln's blockade.

And at it they went, composed of many old clerical rips, who besieged a throne of grace, raising their hands, heaving and setting like an old Tennessee ram at a gate-post, that God would send lightning and storm and raise the blockade. And the Lord did give them a *raise*—at Roanoke Island, and with that kind of lightning and storm which they did not expect in answer to prayer.

In similar vein, the irrepressible Parson contended that another Tennessee preacher claimed Jesus Christ as a Southern man, with all of his apostles good Confederates except the Yankee Judas.[12]

Somewhat more serious were the accusations of R. L. Stanton, professor in the Theological Seminary of the Presbyterian Church in Danville, Kentucky, who published a huge volume to prove that Southern clergymen were responsible for secession and the maintenance of the war. "No complaint need be entered in behalf of those whose conduct we unfold. Least of all will they themselves complain, for they glory in what they have done, and call upon the world to applaud them." Stanton's chief method of exposure was to quote the very words of prominent church leaders in the South, as in the case of T. R. R. Cobb. Early in the war, this Presbyterian from Georgia (later to give his life at Fredericksburg) urged the church to rally its forces behind the Confederacy: "She should not now abandon HER OWN GRAND CREATION. She should not leave the creature of her prayers and labors to the contingencies of the times, or the tender mercies of less concientious patriots. *She should CONSUMMATE what she* has BEGUN."[13]

[12] *Portrait and Biography of Parson Brownlow, the Tennessee Patriot* (Indianapolis, 1862), pp. 44-45.
[13] *Op. cit.*, pp. v-vi, 197-198 (quoted from *Southern Presbyterian* April 20, 1861). In an earlier issue, March 16, 1861, the *Southern Presbyterian* had editorialized: "Will he [a Northern editor] refuse to believe that the Churches of all denominations and the State are AT ONE on the question involved? That as Christian Citizens, THE WHOLE HEART of ministers and people [is] in this matter . . . ? And for the Churches of the whole South, of every denomination, we

The New York *Methodist* placed the blame for this "monstrous treason and terrific war" on Southern members of the church and had the concurrence of Governor Wright of Indiana.[14] Andrew Johnson, having jailed several ministers in Nashville, inquired, *"Who are these reverend traitors, that they should go unpunished for their crimes?"* They were to be disciplined as enemies of society, law and order. "They have poisoned and corrupted boys and silly women, and inculcated rebellion. . . . These men have stolen the livery of heaven to serve the devil in. . . ."[15] The *Daily Nashville Union* agreed with Johnson's sentiments.[16] The Reverend R. C. Grundy, so pro-Confederate that the patriotic Memphis *Appeal* printed one of his sermons in full in May, 1861, but later turned Unionist, wrote to the Memphis *Bulletin* of August 21, 1864: ". . . the southern rebel church . . . is worth more to Mr. Jeff Davis than an army of one hundred thousand drilled and equipped men. . . ." This worthy Lincolnite is also alleged to have said that life was kept in the rebellion by "the clergy, the women and the devil."[17]

In 1862 Jordan Stokes delivered a Fourth of July oration in the hall of the House of Representatives in Nashville, Tennessee. He paid his respects to politicians and editors but reserved his strongest invective for the preachers. According to Stokes, the rebellion

has taken possession bodily of the church and clergy, with now and then an exception, and driven them heedlessly on the broad road toward destruction, presenting to the Chris-

---

indignantly deny that they have been are now, or ever will be, 'the humble and obedient servants of politicians.' No honest man who knows anything of Southern Churches will assert it of them. It is utterly false. He finds 'ministers of the South urging political men to uncompromising resistance.' Just now it was the politicians leading ministers! Yes! And so long as we have tongue or pen to use, we will argue, as duty to God and man, resistance to this unholy crusade against what we believe God's truth, right, duty, honor, and interest."

14 July 6, 1861; Nashville (Tenn.) *Dispatch*, April 10, 1863.

15 *Central Presbyterian*, July 7, 1862.

16 May 11, 1862.

17 Wooten, *op. cit.*, III, 136-147 (June, 1944).

tian world the melancholy spectacle of ministers . . . converting their sacred pulpits into rostrums from which flow fiery tirades of denunciation, sedition, and war to the death, and of churches . . . vieing with each other as to which could dig deepest its pure white robes in the innocent blood of a wicked rebellion, or could furnish the larger number of Generals, Colonels and Captains to lead brother against brother on fields of blood and carnage.[18]

One conclusive proof of the power of the church in its support of the Confederacy may be seen in the efforts of Union generals to take over the appointment of "loyal" ministers and to superintend religious affairs in occupied territory. In most cases difficulties arose because Southern churchmen had been actively engaged in promoting and supporting the war, and continued to voice Confederate sentiments even after their regions were overrun by the enemy.

In the last months of 1863 various orders of Secretary of War Stanton placed Southern Methodist churches with disloyal pastors at the disposal of Northern bishops.[19] Similar action was later taken in regard to Baptist, Presbyterian, and Episcopalian congregations. Disputes arose most often in the liturgical churches in which prayers for the Confederacy or its officials were a part of the service.

As early as the fall of 1861 preachers attending the annual Kentucky Methodist Conference found themselves prisoners of the United States, with the option of taking the oath of allegiance or remaining in custody.[20] Andrew Johnson's dispute with the Nashville clergy has been mentioned —five who refused to subscribe to the oath were sent to Northern prisons.[21] (One of these is supposed to have

[18] *Oration of the Hon. Jordan Stokes . . . delivered in the Hall of the House of Representatives . . .* (Nashville, 1862), pp. 16-17.

[19] Walter L. Fleming (ed.), *Documentary History of Reconstruction, Political, Military, Social, Religious, Educational, and Industrial, 1865 to the Present Time* (Cleveland, 1907), I, 215-216; Edward McPherson, *The Political History of the United States during the Great Rebellion . . .* (Washington, 1865), p. 521.

[20] *Christian Advocate*, Oct. 31, 1861.

[21] Philip M. Hamer, *Tennessee, A History, 1673-1932* (New York, 1935), II, 572-573.

shouted to the crowd as the train pulled out for Louisville: "Don't forget your God, Jeff Davis, and the Southern Confederacy.")[22]   General Grant was embroiled in the same kind of squabbles in Memphis.[23]   This sort of thing became so common that in 1864 the Methodist Episcopal Missionary Society appropriated $35,000 to send ministers into occupied zones "to preach the gospel and Union sentiment."[24]

In Norfolk, Virginia all places of worship were placed at the disposal of the provost marshals, whose powers included the displacement of disloyal ministers.[25]   The Reverend Mr. S. J. P Anderson of St. Louis was found guilty of disloyalty by a military commission and ordered deported within Confederate lines, although the commanding general did not carry out the sentence.[26]   The surveillance of ministers in Missouri was defended by General W. S. Rosecrans, who wrote in April, 1864 that "Most of them have been remarkable for their sympathies with the rebellion, and now live in our midst croaking, fault-finding, and even rejoicing in the nation's struggles and reverses, like the impious son of Noah, who uncovered and mocked the nakedness of his father."[27]   In Alexandria, Virginia, the churches were closed, and in Portsmouth a clergyman was ordered to clean the streets.[28]   Catholic Bishop William H. Elder put up a real fight with occupation authorities in Natchez, Mississippi and this led to his being temporarily deported.[29]

The scraps between General Butler and church leaders in New Orleans became notorious.   Father Ignatius Mullon defied Butler and got away with it.[30]   Some of the churches

[22] Lloyd P. Stryker, *Andrew Johnson: A Study in Courage* (New York, 1929), pp. 98-99.

[23] Robert H. McCaslin, *Presbyterianism in Memphis* (Memphis, n.d.), pp. 54-55.

[24] New York *Christian Advocate and Journal*, Feb. 11, 1864.

[25] Fleming, *Documentary History of Reconstruction*, II, 223.

[26] McPherson, *op. cit.*, pp 537-538.   In his sermon on Jan. 4, 1861 Anderson said, "I may be driven out of this Union" (*op. cit.*, p. 18).

[27] Quoted in McPherson, *op. cit.*, 6. 538.

[28] Cheshire, *op. cit.*, pp. 169-175.

[29] Richmond *Sentinel*, Aug. 25, 1864; Fleming, *Documentary History of Reconstruction*, I, 222-223; Richard O. Gerow, *Cradle Days of St. Mary's at Natchez* (Marrero, La., 1941), pp. 161-165, and *Catholicity in Mississippi* (Marrero, 1939), pp. 61-62.

[30] Baudier, *op. cit.*, p. 427.

were turned over to Northern preachers but this only led to hostile congregations. In Huntsville, Alabama the Reverend Frederick A. Ross was banished by General Rousseau because he had preached a disloyal sermon in which he asked the Lord to bless the enemy and to remove him from the South "as soon as seemeth good in thy sight."[31]   In the same state the Bishop Wilmer episode continued well after Appomattox.[32]   Stubborn opposition of the Southern clergy to military control was undoubtedly motivated, especially after Lee's surrender, as much by the insistence upon separation of church and state as from any love of the Confederacy. For it is difficult to see how the religious leaders or the people themselves, believing as they did in the intervention of the Lord in human affairs, could have come to any other conclusion than that the outcome of the war was God's will.

Evidence involving public opinion in the nineteenth century cannot be neatly summed up on an actuarial basis. It seems reasonable, though, to conclude that, as its greatest social institution, the church in the South constituted the major resource of the Confederacy in the building and maintenance of civilian morale. As no other group, Southern clergymen were responsible for a state of mind which made secession possible, and as no other group they sustained the people in their long, costly and futile War for Southern Independence.

[31] Fleming, *Civil War and Reconstruction in Alabama* (New York, 1905), p. 229.
[32] *Ibid.*, pp. 327-330, and Fleming, *Documentary History of Reconstruction*, I, 223-236.

Bibliography

Books and Articles

A Few Historic Records of the Church in the Diocese of Texas, During the Rebellion. Together with a Correspondence Between the Right Rev. Alexander Gregg, D. D., and the Rev. Charles Gillette. New York, 1865.

Baudier, Roger. *The Catholic Church in Louisiana.* New Orleans, 1939.

Bettersworth, John K. *Confederate Mississippi.* Baton Rouge, 1943.

Blied, Benjamin J. *Catholics and the Civil War.* Milwaukee, 1945.

Boyd, Jesse L. *A Popular History of the Baptists in Mississippi.* Jackson, 1930.

[Boykin, S.] *History of the Baptist Denomination in Georgia.* Atlanta, 1881.

Bryan, T. Conn. "The Churches in Georgia During the Civil War," *Georgia Historical Quarterly,* XXXIII, 283-302 (Dec. 1949).

Carroll, J. M. *A History of the Texas Baptists. . . .* Dallas, 1923.

Cauthen, Charles E. *South Carolina Goes to War, 1860-1861.* Chapel Hill, 1950.

Chestnut, Mary Boykin. *A Diary from Dixie.* New York, 1905.

Cheshire, Joseph B. *The Church in the Confederate States: A History of the Protestant Episcopal Church in the Confederate States.* New York, 1912.

Christian, John T. *History of the Baptists of Louisiana.* Nashville, 1923.

Coffin, Charles C. *Four Years of Fighting.* . . . Boston, 1866.

Cooper, William R. "Parson Brownlow: A Study of Reconstruction in Tennessee," *Southwestern Bulletin*, XIX, 6-7 (Dec., 1931).

Coulter, E. Merton. *The Confederate States of America, 1861-1865.* Baton Rouge, 1950.

————, ed. Ulrich B. Phillips, *The Course of the South to Secession.* New York, 1939.

Cross, Joseph. *Camp and Field: Papers from the Portfolio of an Army Chaplain.* Macon, 1864.

DesChamps, Margaret B. "Benjamin Morgan Palmer, Orator-Preacher of the Confederacy," *Southern Speech Journal*, XIX, 14-22 (Sept., 1953).

Fleming, Walter L. *Civil War and Reconstruction in Alabama.* New York, 1905.

————, ed. *Documentary History of Reconstruction, Political, Military, Social, Religious, Educational, and Industrial, 1865 to the Present Time.* Cleveland, 1907.

————. "The Churches of Alabama During the Civil War and Reconstruction," *Gulf States Historical Magazine*, I, 105-127 (July, 1902).

Fletcher W. A. *Rebel Private, Front and Rear.* Beaumont, 1908.

Fuller, Erasmus Q. *An Appeal to the Records: A Vindication of the Methodist Episcopal Church, in Its Policy and Proceedings Toward the South.* Cincinnati, 1876.

Gerish, Theodore and John Hutchinson. *The Blue and the Gray.* Bangor, 1884.

Gerow, Richard O. *Catholicity in Mississippi.* Marrero, La., 1939.

————. *Cradle Days of St. Mary's at Natchez.* Marrero, La., 1941.

Hamer, Philip M. *Tennessee, A History, 1673-1932.* New York, 1935.

Hoge, Peyton H. *Moses Drury Hoge: Life and Letters.* Richmond, 1899.

[Hopley, Catherine C.] *Life in the South from the Commencement of the War, By a British Subject.* London 1863.

Hutchinson, John. See Theodore Gerish.

Jones, Benjamin W. *Under the Stars and Bars: A History of the Surry Light Artillery.* Richmond, 1909.

Kibler, Lillian A. *Benjamin Franklin Perry: South Carolina Unionist.* Durham, 1946.

Logan, John R. *Sketches of the Broad River and King's Mountain Baptist Association. . . .* Shelby, 1887.

McCaslin, Robert H. *Presbyterianism in Memphis.* Memphis, n. d.

McPherson, Edward. *The Political History of the United States during the Great Rebellion. . . .* Washington, 1865.

Martin, Bessie. *Desertion of Alabama Troops from the Confederate Army: A Study in Sectionalism.* New York, 1932.

Moore, Albert B. *Conscription and Conflict in the Confederacy.* New York, 1924.

Naff, George E. "Cleveland's Text Books," *Quarterly Review of the Methodist Episcopal Church, South,* XV, 63-75 (Jan., 1861).

Phillips,Ulrich B. See E. Merton Coulter.

Pollard, Edward A. *The Second Year of the War.* Richmond, 1863.

Portrait and Biography of Parson Brownlow, the Tennessee Patriot. Indianapolis, 1862.

Price, R. N. *Holston Methodism.* Nashville, 1913.

Stanton, R. L. *The Church and the Rebellion: A Consideration of the Rebellion against the Government of the United States; and the Agency of the Church, North and South, in Relation thereto.* New York, 1864.

Stryker, Lloyd P. *Andrew Jackson: A Study in Courage.* New York, 1929.

Sweet, William W. *Methodism in American History.* Cincinnati, 1933.

———. *The Methodist Episcopal Church and the Civil War.* Cincinnati, 1912.

———. *The Story of Religions in America.* New York, 1930.

Vander Velde, Lewis G. *The Presbyterian Churches and the Federal Union, 1861-1864.* Cambridge, 1932.

Vandiver, Frank E., ed. *The Civil War Diary of General Josiah Gorgas.* University, Ala., 1947.

Walmsley, James E., cont. "Documents—The Change of Secession Sentiment in Virginia in 1861," *American Historical Review,* XXXI, 82-101 (Oct., 1925).

Wiley, Bell I. " 'Holy Joes' of the Sixties: A Study of Civil War Chaplains," *Huntington Library Quarterly,* XVI, 287-304 (May, 1953).

———. "The Movement to Humanize the Institution of Slavery during the Confederacy," *Emory University Quarterly,* V, 207-220 (Dec., 1949).

———. *Southern Negroes, 1861-1865.* New Haven, 1938.

Wooten, Fred T. "Religious Activities in Civil War Memphis," *Tennessee Historical Quarterly,* III, 135-136 (June, 1944).

Sermons and Pamphlets

Address of the Atlanta Register to the People of the Confederate States. Atlanta, 1864.

Address to Christians Throughout the World: By the Clergy of the Confederate States of America. London, 1863.

Anderson, S. P. J. *The Dangers and Duties of the Present Crisis.* . . . St. Louis, 1861.

Atkinson, J. M. *God the Giver of Victory and Peace.* . . . Raleigh, 1862.

Atkinson, Thomas. *Christian Duty in the Present Time of Trouble.* . . . Wilmington, 1861.

Burrows, J. L. *The New Richmond Theatre.* . . . Richmond, 1863.

Caldwell, John H. *Slavery and Southern Methodism.* . . . Newnan, Ga., 1865.

Dabney, R. L. *The Christian Soldier.* . . . Richmond, 1862.

Doggett, David S. *A Nation's Ebenezer.* . . . Richmond, 1862.

Dreher, Daniel I. *A Sermon.* . . . Salisbury, 1861.

Elliott, J. H. *The Bloodless Victory: A Sermon Preached. . . on the Occasion of Taking Fort Sumter.* Charleston, 1861.

Elliott, Stephen. *A Sermon Preached in Christ Church, Savannah. . . April, 1864.* Macon, 1864.

———. *Ezra's Dilemma.* . . . Savannah, 1863.

———. *Funeral Services at the Burial of the Right Rev. Leonidas Polk.* . . . Columbia, 1864.

———. *God's Presence with the Confederate States.* . . . Savannah, 1861.

———. *God's Presence with Our Army at Manassas.* . . . Savannah, 1861.

———. *How to Renew Our National Strength.* . . . Savannah, 1861.

———. *"New Wine Not To Be Put in Old Bottles." A Sermon Preached in Christ Church, Savannah.* . . . Savannah, 1862.

———. *Our Cause in Harmony with the Purposes of God in Jesus Christ.* . . . Savannah, 1862.

———. *"Samson's Riddle." A Sermon*. . . . Macon, 1863.

———. *Sermon Preached in Christ's Church, Savannah, September 18, 1862*. Savannah, 1862.

———. *The Silver Trumpets of the Sanctuary*. . . . Savannah, 1861.

———. *"Vain Is the Help of Man." A Sermon*. . . . Macon, 1864.

Finley, I. R. *The Lord Reigneth*, Richmond, 1863.

Gregg, Alexander. *The Duties Growing Out of It, and the Benefits To Be from the Present War*. Austin, 1861.

Hoffmeister, J. M. *Come to the Rescue*. . . . Lynchburg, 1863.

Hoge, William J. *Sketch of Dabney Carr Harrison*. . . . Richmond, 1863.

Lee, LeRoy M. *Our Country—Our Dangers—Our Duty*. . . . Richmond, 1863.

McIntosh, William H. *James C. Sumner, The Young Soldier Ready for Death*. . . . Marion, Ala., 1862.

Mangum, Adolphus W. *Myrtle Leaves; or Tokens at the Tomb*. Raleigh, 1864.

Meade, William. *Address on the Day of Fasting and Prayer*. . . . Richmond, 1861.

Michelbacher, M. J. *A Sermon Delivered . . . at the German Hebrew Synagogue "Bayth Ahabah."* Richmond, 1863.

Miles, James W. *God in History. A Discourse Delivered Before the Graduating Class of the College of Charleston*. . . . Charleston, 1863.

Minnigerode, Charles. *"He that believeth shall not make haste." A Sermon*. . . . Richmond, 1865.

Mitchell, J. C. *Fast Day Sermon*. . . . Mobile, 1861.

Moore, Hannah. *Parley the Porter, An Allegory*. Richmond, 186-.

Moore, Thomas V. *Discourse before the Congregations of the First and Second Presbyterian Churches, Richmond, November 15, 1861.* Richmond, 1861.

―――. *God Our Refuge and Strength in This War. . . .* Richmond, 1861.

Moore, W. D. *The Life and Works of Col. Henry Hughes; A Funeral Sermon. . . .* Mobile, 1863.

Palmer, Benjamin M. *A Discourse before the General Assembly of South Carolina. . . .* Columbia, 1864.

―――. *National Responsibility Before God. . . .* New Orleans, 1861.

―――. *The Oath of Allegiance to the United States Discussed in Its Moral and Political Bearings.* Richmond, 1863.

―――. "Thanksgiving Day Discourse; Delivered in the First Presbyterian Church, New Orleans, November 29, 1860," *DeBow's Review,* XXX, 324-326 (Feb., 1861).

―――. *A Vindication of Secession and the South. . . .* Columbia, 1861.

Paris, John. *A Sermon: Preached Before Brig. Gen. Hoke's Brigade . . . upon the Death of Twenty-Two Men, Who Had Been Executed in the Presence of the Brigade for the Crime of Treason.* Greensborough, 1864.

Physician. *Liquor and Lincoln.* Petersburg, 186-.

Pierce, George F. *The Word of God A Nation's Life. . . .* Augusta, 1862.

Pierce, Henry N. *Sermon Preached in St. John's Church, Mobile. . . .* Mobile, 1861.

Pinckney, Charles Cotesworth. *Nebuchadnezzar's Fault and Fall. . . .* Charleston, 1861.

[Polk, Leonidas.] *General Polk's Report of the Battle of Belmont.* Columbus, Ky., 1861.

Presbyterian Committee of Publication. *Tract No. 3.* n. p., n. d.

Ramsey, James B. *True Eminence Found in Holiness.* . . .
Lynchburg, 1863.

Randolph, Alfred M. *Address on the Day of Fasting and
Prayer.* . . . Fredericksburg, 1861.

Reed, Edward. *A People Saved by the Lord.* . . . Charleston, 1861.

Renfroe, J. J. D. *"The Battle is God's." A Sermon.* . . .
Richmond, 1863.

Renfroe, Nathaniel D. *A Model Confederate Soldier.* Richmond, 1863.

Sermons of Bishop Pierce and Rev. B. M. Palmer . . . Before the General Assembly. . . . Milledgeville, 1863.

Smyth, Thomas. *The Battle of Fort Sumter: Its Mystery
and Miracle: God's Mystery and Mercy.* Columbia, 1861.

———. *The Sin and the Curse; or the Union, The True
Source of Disunion, and Our Duty in the Present Crisis.*
Charleston, 1860.

Stiles, Joseph C. *Capt. Thomas E. King; or, A Word to the
Army and the Country.* Charleston, 1864.

———. *National Rectitude the only True Basis of National
Prosperity; An Appeal to the Confederate States.* Petersburg, 1863.

[Stokes, Jordan.] *Oration of . . . delivered in the Hall of
the House of Representatives.* . . . Nashville, 1862.

Thornwell, James H. *Fast Day Sermons, or The Pulpit on
the State of the Nation.* New York, 1861.

———. *The State of the Country.* . . . Columbia, 1861.

Tucker, Henry. *God in the War.* . . . Milledgeville, 1861.

Tucker, John Randolph. *The Southern Church Justified in
Its Support of the South in the Present War.* Richmond,
1863.

Tucker, J. W. *God Sovereign and Man Free.* . . . Fayetteville, 1862.

Wiley, Calvin H. *Circular to the People of North Carolina.*
Greensboro, 1863.

————. *Scriptural Views of National Trials.* Greensboro,
1863.

Wilmer, Richard H. *Future Good—The Explanation of
Present Reserves.* . . . Charlotte, 1864.

Winkler, Edward T. *Duties of the Citizen Soldier.* . . .
Charleston, 1861.

Church and Government Publications

*Acts and Resolutions of the Third Session of the Provi-
sional Congress of the Confederate States of America.*
. . . Richmond, 1861.

*Acts of the General Assembly of the State of Georgia . . .
1862, and Extra Session of 1863.* Milledgeville, 1863.

*Journal of the Forty-Fifth Annual Convention of the Pro-
testant Episcopal Church in the State of North Carolina.* . . . n. p., 1862.

*Journal of the Proceedings of the Convention of the People
of Florida.* . . . Tallahassee, 1861.

*Journal of the Protestant Episcopal Convention, Diocese of
Mississippi.* Jackson, 1865.

*Journal of the Thirty-Fifth Annual Convention of the Pro-
testant Episcopal Church in the Diocese of Mississippi.*
Jackson, 1861.

*Journal of the Sixty-Eighth Annual Convention of the Pro-
testant Episcopal Church in Virginia.* . . . Richmond,
1863.

*Journal of the 13th Annual Convention of the Protestant
Episcopal Church in the Diocese of Texas.* . . . Houston,
1862.

*Minutes of the . . . Annual Meeting of the Dover Baptist
Association.* . . [1862-1866]. Richmond, 1866.

Minutes of the Baptist Convention of the State of Georgia [1861, 1863, 1864]. Macon, 1861, 1863, Atlanta, 1864.

Minutes of the Baptist General Association of Virginia [1862, 1863, 1864]. Richmond, 1863, 1864, Petersburg, 1863.

Minutes of the Evangelical Lutheran Synod [and Ministerium] of South Carolina [1862, 1864]. Columbia, 1862. 1864.

Minutes of the Fifty-Fifth Anniversary of the Mississippi Baptist Association. . . 1861. n. p., n. d.

Minutes of the Forty-Second Anniversary of the State Convention of the Baptist Denomination in S. C. Columbia, 1862.

Minutes of the Forty-Eighth [and Forty-Ninth] Sessions of the Presbyterian Synod of North Carolina. . . . Fayetteville, 1862, 1863.

Minutes of the [Presbyterian] Synod of Virginia. . . . [1861, 1862, 1863]. Richmond, 1861, 1862, 1863,

Minutes of the Second Convention of the General Synod of the Evangelical Lutheran Church. . . . Savannah, 1864.

Minutes of the Thirty-Fourth Annual Session of the Columbus Baptist Association. Columbus, 1862.

Proceedings of a Convention of Delegates from Various Presbyteries in the Southern States of America. Atlanta, 1861.

Proceedings of the Twenty-Second Annual Meeting of the Domestic Missionary Society of Richmond. . . . Richmond, 1861.

Proceedings of the Southern Baptist Convention. . . May 10-13, 1861. Richmond, 1861.

War of the Rebellion: A Compilation of the Official Records of the Union and Confederate Armies. Washington, 1880-1891. 128 vols.

Newspapers

Augusta *Daily Chronicle and Sentinel;* Augusta *Register;* *Army and Navy Messenger* (Petersburg, Va.) ; *Biographical Pen* (Lynchburg, Va.) ; *Central Presbyterian* (Richmond) ; Charleston *Mercury; Christian Advocate* (Nashville) ; *Christian Observer and Presbyterian Witness* (Richmond) ; *Church Intelligencer* (Raleigh) ; *Free Witness* (New Orleans) ; Greensborough (N. C.) *Patriot;* Lynchburg (Va.) *Weekly Register;* Memphis *Daily Appeal;* Mobile *Register and Advertiser;* Montgomery *Weekly Mail;* Nashville *Daily Union;* Nashville *Dispatch;* Nashville *Republican Banner;* Petersburg (Va.) *Daily Express; Religious Herald* (Richmond) ; Richmond *Dispatch;* Richmond *Enquirer;* Richmond *Examiner;* Richmond *Sentinel; Southern Episcopalian* (Charleston) ; *Southern Presbyterian* (Columbia) ; Tallahassee *Florida Sentinel;* Thomasville (Ga.) *Southern Enterprise.*

Miscellaneous

Journal of the Rio Grande Mission Conference, 1859-1865. MS, in University of Texas Library, Austin.

Letters of Albert H. Clark, in possession of Mrs. Calvin Brown, Oxford, Miss.

Letters of Lewis Burwell and others, in Brock Collection, Henry E. Huntington Library, San Marino, Calif.

Letters of William C. Chambers, S. M. Wood, J. A. Morris and J. H. Chambers, 1862. Typescript in University of Texas Library, Austin.

Minute Book of Elon Baptist Church, Hanover, Virginia, 1861-1865. MS, in University of Richmond Library.

Minutes of the Lexington Presbytery, 1860-1865. MS, in Union Theological Seminary, Richmond, Va.

Miscellaneous pamphlets and leaflets in Curry Pamphlets Collection (vol. XXXIV), Alabama State Department of Archives and History, Montgomery.

Mississippi Governor's Records, 1861-1865. MSS, in Mississippi Department of Archives and History, Jackson.

Palestine Baptist Church Record, Sept., 1856-June, 1936. MS, in Mississippi College Library, Clinton.

Snipes, David F. "The Churches and Public Opinion in the Confederacy," unpublished thesis, 1948, University of Mississippi Library, University.

Wiley, Calvin H., Papers, in North Carolina Department of Archives and History, Raleigh.

Index

A

Abolitionism, 9, 22, 23, 47, 51, 58, 69, 70, 87
Adams, Abigail, 81
Address to Christians Throughout the World, 50
Alabama, 18, 60, 80, 88
Alexandria, Va., 47, 100
American Bible Society, 77
American Revolution, 25, 32, 38, 59
An Impressive Summons, 57
Anderson, L. B., 75, 76
Anderson, Samuel J. P., 26, 100
Andrew, James O., 87
Annan, John E., 23
Appomatox, 40, 65, 101
Archie's Tennessee Brigade, 80
"Are You Ready to Die?", 95
Arkansas, 88
Army and Navy Messenger, 52, 58, 61
Atkinson, Joseph M., 33
Atkinson, Mr., 77
Atkinson, Thomas, 21, 22, 26
Atlanta, Ga., 54, 56, 83
Atlanta (Ga.) *Commonwealth*, 26
Aughey, John H., 20
Augusta, Ga., 18, 57
Augusta (Ga.) *Chronicle and Sentinel*, 38
Augusta (Ga.) *Register*, 89
Austin, Texas, 48, 70

B

Baltimore, Md., 28, 46, 85, 89
Baldwin, S. D., 50
Baptist Church, 16, 18, 21, 28, 34, 38, 42, 44, 45, 49, 54, 60, 61, 62, 66, 67, 69, 70, 71, 73, 75, 76, 79, 80, 90, 96, 99
Baptist Committee on the State of the Country, 28, 66
Baptist General Association of Virginia, 45, 54

Baton Rouge, La., 95
Beauregard, Pierre G. T., 85, 88
Beecher, Henry Ward, 16, 86, 87
Bedford County, Va., 48
Bell, Mrs., 89
Belmont, Battle of, 33
Benefits We Enjoy as a Nation, 21
Bethel, 14
Bewley, Anthony, 20
Biographical Pen, 86
Black, Mr., 88
Blanton, Lindsay H., 23
Bocock, John H., 23
Boston (Mass.) *Freedman*, 87
Boyd, A. H., 21
Bragg, Braxon, 92
Bragg, Thomas, 77
Breckinridge, Robert J., 22
Bridge Street Presbyterian Church (Georgetown, D.C.), 23
Broad River Baptist Association (N. C.), 75
Brown, Joseph E., 60
Brownlow, William G., 20, 96
Buchanan, James, 26
Burnside, Ambrose E., 97
Burrows, John L., 68
Burwell, Lewis, 13
Butler, Benjamin F., 79, 100

C

Caldwell, John H., 41
Calhoun, John C., 16
Capernaum Baptist Church (N. C.), 75
Carey, Miss., 89
Carrington, Phram, 56
Caskey, Thomas W., 17
Catholic Church, 28, 48, 78, 79, 100
Central Presbyterian (Richmond, Va.), 18, 21, 48, 59, 61, 79, 81, 83, 85, 94
Central Presbyterian Church (St. Louis, Mo.), 26

Chancellorsville, Battle of, 32, 36, 65
Chaplains, 87
Charleston, S. C., 14, 17, 26, 44, 48, 55, 66, 71
Charleston, Tenn., 69
Charleston (S. C.) *Courier*, 69
Charleston (S. C.) *Mercury*, 60, 89
Charlottesville, Va., 23
Chattanooga, Battle of, 32
Chester, S. C., 15
Chestnut, Mary Boykin, 54
Chickamauga, Battle of, 32, 57, 65, 92
Child's Index, 91
Christ Church (Houston, Texas), 28
Christ Church (Savannah, Ga.), 31
Christian Advocate (Nashville, Tenn.), 19, 58, 79, 87
Christian Banner (Boston, Mass.), 86
Christian Church, 17
Christian Index, 54
Christian Observer and Presbyterian Witness (Richmond, Va.), 19, 36, 39, 44, 52, 54, 59, 65, 67, 70, 73, 80, 81, 83, 85, 92
The Christian Soldier, 56
Church Intelligencer (Raleigh, N. C.), 36, 40, 60, 71
Church of the Holy Communion (Charleston, S. C.), 55
Cincinnati (Ohio) *Commercial*, 77
Claiborne County, Miss., 56
Clark, Albert H., 13
Cobb, Howell, 55
Cobb, Thomas R. R., 97
Cold Harbor, Battle of, 32
Columbia, S. C., 90
Columbus, Ga., 43
Columbus (Ga.) Baptist Association, 93
Columbus, Miss., 19
Columbus, Ohio, 22
Confederate Congress, 45, 52, 64, 73, 96
Confederate States of America, 22, 37, 45, 61, 73
Converse, Amasa, 83
Crandall, Marjorie Lyle, 10
Crawfordsville, Miss., 65
Cross, Joseph, 40, 84
Cumberland Presbyterian Church (Memphis, Tenn.), 32

D

Dabney, Robert L., 30, 56, 77
Dance, Mathew, 30
Danville, Ky., 97
Danville [Ky.] Quarterly Review, 22
Davis, C. A., 32
Davis, Jefferson, 19, 21, 28, 30, 31, 34, 35, 45, 47, 48, 55, 60, 61, 62, 64, 79, 85, 88, 93, 95, 98, 100
Davis, Josiah, 86, 87
Davis, Thomas F., 21
"The Defence of Our Country a Christian Duty," 48
Dickinson, A. E., 43, 74
Diocesan Missionary Society, 73
Doggett, David S., 33
Dover (Va.) Baptist Association, 70, 80
Dreher, Daniel I., 26, 82
"Duties of the Hour," 54

E

Eagleton, George, 89
Early, John, 75
East Alabama Baptist Convention, 60
Elder, William H., 48, 100
Elizabethtown, N. J., 23
Elliott, J. H., 31
Elliott, Stephen, 25, 31, 34, 35, 36, 43, 45, 58, 49, 53, 54, 57, 64, 81, 96
Elon (Va.) Baptist Church, 75
Emancipation Proclamation, 86
Emory College, 84
Episcopal Church, 21, 28, 44, 59, 61, 90, 96, 99
Episcopalian Council in Virginia, 44
Evangelical Lutheran Synod, 72
Evangelical Lutheran Synod of South Carolina, 29
Evangelical Society of Petersburg, 53
Extortion, 31, 37, 50, 70-72

F

Fast Days, 21, 22, 31, 32, 34, 36, 45, 64-69, 95
Finacune, John, 79
First Presbyterian Church (Columbus, Miss.), 19
Fitzgerald, Mr., 77
Fitzhugh, George, 84
Fletcher, W. A., 95

Florida, 17, 86
Fort McHenry, 46
Fort Donelson, Battle of, 32, 56
Fort Sumter, 21, 31, 36, 44, 79, 82
Fortress Monroe, 47
Fort Worth, Texas, 20
Forrest, Nathan B., 36
Fredericksburg, Battle of, 32, 68, 90, 97

G

Georgetown, D. C., 23
Georgia, 18, 29, 35, 38, 48, 54, 55, 61, 69, 70, 79, 80, 88, 97
Georgia Assembly, 29, 35
Georgia Bapist Association, 69
Georgia Methodist Conference, 18
Gettysburg, Battle of, 32, 36, 62, 65, 71, 74, 92
Gholson, Thomas S., 70
"Gideon," 69
Gonzales, Texas, 18
Goodrich, Dr., 78
Gorgas, Josiah, 65, 71
Grace Church (Charleston, S. C.), 44
Grand Gulf, Miss., 36
Grant, Ulysses S., 33, 39, 54, 66, 91, 92, 100
Green, William Mercer, 43, 61
Greensboro, N. C., 71
Gregg, Alexander, 21, 28, 48, 50, 70
Grier, M. B., 22
Grundy, R. C., 98

H

Hall, Mr., 78
Hampden-Sidney College, 77
Hampton, Va., 47
Hanks, Hannah, 84
Hardee, William J., 77
Harpers' Weekly (New York), 85
Harrison, Dabney, 56
Higgins, Dr., 43
Hoffmeister, Jonathan M., 67
Hoge, Moses D., 49, 62, 80
Hoge, William J., 23
Holly Springs, Miss., 59
Holston (Tenn.) Methodist Conference, 75
Hood, John B., 77
Hooker, Joseph(36
Houston, Texas, 28
Hoyt, Thomas A., 22
Hughes, Henry, 56
Huntsville, Ala., 101

J

Jackson, Miss., 17, 43, 56, 77
Jackson (Miss.) *Daily Mississippian,* 78
Jackson, J. W., 86
Jackson, Thomas, J., 32, 35
James, Mr., 77
Johnson, Andrew, 98, 99
Johnston, Joseph E., 77, 92
Jones, Benjamin W., 67
Jones, J., 26
Jones, Sarah, 76

K

Kendrick, J. R., 46
Kentucky, 22, 23, 47
Kentucky Methodist Conference, 99
King, Thomas E., 57
Kings Mountain (N. C.) Baptist Association, 70
Kingsley, Brother, 19
Kinston, N. C., 76
Kirk, Dr., 86
Knoxville, Tenn., 34, 96
Knoxville (Tenn.) *Whig,* 20

L

"The Landing of the Pilgrims," 91
Lancaster, S. C., 15
Lane, W. T., 76
Lebanon, Ky., 79
Leacock, Dr., 78
Lee, LeRoy M., 37, 89
Lee, Robert E., 32, 33, 38, 39, 64, 71, 91, 92, 101
Lexington, Battle of, 28
Lexington (Va.) Presbytery, 40
Leyburn, George W., 22
Lincoln, Abraham, 16, 20, 23, 30, 32, 39, 46, 67, 84, 85, 90, 97, 98
Lincoln, Mary Todd, 59
Longstreet, James, 90
Lonn, Ella, 7
Lord, W. W., 73, 78
Louisiana, 54, 57, 60, 73, 89
Louisville, Ky., 100
Lutheran Church, 21, 29, 36, 72
Lutheran Synod of South Carolina, 36
Lynch, Patrick, 48
Lynchburg, Va., 37
Lyon, James A., 19

M

McClellan, George B., 13, 83
McGill, John, 77, 82, 96

Macon, Ga., 14
Macon, Miss., 20
McPheeters, Samuel B., 23
McRae, Thaddeus, 95
Malvern Hill, Battle of, 32, 68
Manassas, First or Second Battle of, 14, 15, 31, 32, 57, 65, 82, 85, 88
Mangum, Lieut., 14
Marathon, Battle of, 58
Marshall, Dr., 43
Marshall, Mr., 78
Martin, Augustus, 28, 48
Martin, Joseph H., 34
Massachusetts, 28
Meade, William, 21, 38, 39
Memphis, Tenn., 32, 73, 100
Memphis (Tenn.) *Bulletin*, 98
Memphis (Tenn.) *Daily Appeal*, 20, 54, 98
Mercer University, 29
Methodist (New York), 98
Methodist Church, 16, 18, 20, 21, 61, 75, 89, 96, 99, 100
Methodist Episcopal Missionary Society, 100
Methodist Rio Grande Mission Conference (Texas), 61
Michelberger, Maximillian J., 50
Middle District Baptist Association (Va.), 62
Miles, James W., 26
Miles, William Porcher, 96
Milledgeville, Ga., 89
Miller, Willis L., 77
Minnigerode, Charles, 39, 55
Missouri, 22, 23, 47, 100
Michell, J. C., 29
Mobile, Ala., 29, 60
A Model Confederate Soldier, 56
Montgomery, Ala., 21, 74
Montgomery (Ala.) Guards, 77
Montgomery (Ala.) *Weekly Mail*, 89
Moore, Albert B., 7
Moore, Hannah, 73
Moore, Thomas V., 29, 82
Moore, William D., 56
Moulton, Ala., 36
"Mrs. D.", 90
Mullon, Ignatius, 100

N

Nashville, Tenn., 50, 58, 73, 79, 84, 85, 98, 99
Nashville [Tenn.] *Daily Union*, 98

Natchez, Miss., 48, 87, 100
Natchitoches, La., 28, 48
New Market, Tenn., 89
New Orleans, La., 17, 28, 67, 73, 78, 79, 80, 85, 94, 100
New Orleans (La.) Confederate Guards, 27
New Orleans (La.) *Daily Delta*, 17
New Orleans (La.) *True Witness*, 28
New Richmond (Va.) Theatre, 68
New York, N. Y., 23
New York *Times*, 90
Newnan, Ga., 41
Newport, Ky., 88
Norfolk, Va., 100
North Carolina, 29, 50, 61, 67, 76, 80, 84, 88
North Carolina Presbyterian Synod, 50, 80
Northern Church, 15, 17, 28, 29, 57, 99-101

O

"O Chosen Leader in the Cause of Right," 61
Oath of Allegiance, 72-74, 78-79
Oath of Allegiance, 73
Odin, Jean, 67
Oglethorpe (Ga.) Rifles, 14
Otey, James H., 21
Oxford, Miss., 13
Owsley, Frank L., 7

P

Paine, Thomas, 17
Palestine (Miss.) Baptist Church, 75
Palmer, Benjamin Morgan, 16, 17, 21, 22, 27, 37, 42, 43, 52, 54, 73, 74, 78, 86, 95
Paris, John, 76
Parley the Porter, An Allegory, 73
Pennsylvania, 92
Perkins, John, 73
Perry, Benjamin Franklin, 18
Pettus, John J., 65
Petersburg, Va., 14, 52, 70
Phelan, James, 20
Philadelphia, Pa., 22, 86
Pickens, Francis W., 96
Pierce, George F., 28, 35, 43, 55, 77
Pierce, Henry N., 29
Pinckney, Charles Cotesworth, 44

Pine Mountain, Battle of, 57
Plymouth Church (New York), 86
Polk, Leonidas L., 33, 56, 57, 60, 77
Pollard, Edward A., 60
Porter, Robert K., 55
Portsmouth, Va., 100
"Prayer of the Extortioner," 71
Presbyterian Church, 16, 18, 19, 20, 21, 22, 29, 30, 34, 40, 44, 48, 50, 55, 72, 73, 77, 79, 80, 86, 94, 96, 97, 99
Presbyterian Synod of North Carolina, 29
Presbyterian Synod of South Carolina, 18
Presbyterian Synod of Virginia, 34, 44
Price, Sterling, 23, 54
Pulaski (Tenn.) Guards, 45

Q

Quakers, 89, 93
Quence, Mr., 76
Quinlan, John, 60

R

"The Rainbow Round the Throne," 42
Raleigh (N. C.) *Standard*, 60
Ramsey, James B., 35
Randolph, Alfred M., 28
Read, Dr., 28
Religious Herald (Richmond, Va.), 19, 34 ,40, 50, 62, 66, 70, 71, 80, 86, 87, 89
Renfroe, J. J. D., 43, 62, 74
Renfroe, Nathaniel D., 56
Rhett, Robert Barnwell, 16
Richmond, Va., 13, 14, 19, 33, 40, 50, 54, 60, 62, 68, 83
Richmond (Va.) College, 13
Richmond (Va.) *Dispatch*, 96
Richmond (Va.) *Examiner*, 60, 89, 94
Richmond (Va.) *Whig*, 66, 85
Roanoke Island, N. C., 97
Robinson, Stuart, 22
Rome, Ga., 26
Rosecrans, William S., 100
Ross, Dr., 52
Ross, Frederick A., 100
Rousseau, Lovell H., 101
Rutherford, Edward H., 78
Rutledge, Francis H., 17, 21

S

Savannah, Ga., 17, 31
Scott, Jackson, 74
Scott, Winfield S., 46
Scriptural Views of National Trials, 69
Second Chronicles, 27, 66
"The Sentinel," 94
Secession, ,8, 16, 19, 21, 23, 24, 27, 93
Seven Days Battle, 65
Seven Pines, Battle of, 61
Sharpsburg, Battle of, 56
Shaver, David, 40
Sherman, William T., 15, 54, 78, 91
Shepperson, J. G., 48
"Sinner, You Are Soon to be Damned!", 95
Sixth North Carolina Regiment, 14
Skinner, Mr., 77
Slavery, 15, 17, 20, 25, 28, 34, 51, 56, 68-69, 84
The Slavery Conflict and Its Effect on the Church, 41
Smedes, Mr., 77
Smith, Edmund Kirby, 54
Smyth, Thomas, 17, 26, 30, 46, 51,
South Carolina, 16, 18, 19, 20, 21, 22, 27, 29, 36, 37, 52, 79, 86, 88, 96
South Carolina Convention, 19
South Carolina Legislature, 37, 52
Southern Advocate, 58
Southern Baptist, 77
Southern Baptist Convention, 60
Southern Christian Advocate (Charleston and Columbia, S. C.), 83
Southern Churchman (Richmond, Va.), 65
Southern Episcopalian (Charleston, S. C.), 15, 61
Southern Lutheran (Charleston and Columbia, S. C.), 30, 59
Southern Presbyterian (Columbia, S. C.), 19, 97
Southern Presbyterian General Assembly, 20
Southern Presbyterian Review (Columbia, S. C.), 30, 51
South Western Baptist (Tuskegee, Ala.), 82
Sparta, Ga., 77

St. Andrew's Church (Jackson, Miss.), 43
St. David's Church (Austin, Texas), 70
St. Louis, Mo., 19, 23, 47, 100
Stanton, Edward M., 99
Stanton, Robert L., 22, 86, 97
States Rights, 19, 20, 23
Stephens, Alexander H., 59
Stiles, Joseph C., 37, 57
Stokes, Jordan, 98
Strong River (Miss.) Baptist Association, 71
Summers, Dr., 58
Sumner, Charles, 16

T

Tallahassee *Florida Sentinel*, 50
Taylor, Richard, 54
Tennessee, 92, 97, 98
Tennessee Legislature, 98
Texas, 20, 47, 49, 95
Thomasville (N. C.) Rifles, 77
Thornwell, James H., 16, 17, 58, 83, 86
True Presbyterian (Louisville, Ky.), 22
Tucker, Henry H., 29, 65
Tucker, J. W., 77
Tucker, John Randolph, 61, 62
Tuskegee Baptist Association (Ala.), 80
Twelfth Mississippi Regiment, 80
Tydings, R. M., 69

U

Union Theological Seminary, 77
Union Baptist Association of Texas, 49
United Presbyterians (Va.), 30

V

Vance, Zebulon B., 70
Verot, Augustine, 17
Versailles, Ky., 23
Vicksburg, Battle of, 32
Vicksburg, Miss., 36, 65, 73, 78, 89, 90, 92, 94
Vigilantes, 20
Virginia, 30, 33, 34, 40, 44, 45, 47, 54, 55, 62, 66, 67, 70, 73, 75, 76, 78, 79, 86, 90, 92

W

The War of the South Vindicated, 51
Washington, George, 59, 70
Washington, Va., 47
Watson, Mr., 52
Whittier, John G., 16
Wiley, Calvin H., 69, 84
Wiley, E. E., 75
Wilmer, Richard H., 38, 74, 101
Wilmington, N. C., 21, 22
Wilson, James C., 18
Winchester, Va., 21
Winkler, Edward T., 29
Woodbridge, George, 61
Wright, George G., 98

Y

Yancey, William Lowndes, 16
Yankeeism, 82
Young Men's Christian Association, 28, 62

American History Titles in
THE NORTON LIBRARY

SAMUEL FLAGG BEMIS
   The Latin American Policy of the
      United States   N412

FAWN BRODIE
   Thaddeus Stevens   N331

ROBERT E. BROWN
   Charles Beard and the Constitution   N296

EDMUND CODY BURNETT
   The Continental Congress   N278

DUDLEY TAYLOR CORNISH
   The Sable Arm: Negro Troops in the
      Union Army, 1861-1865   N334

JOHN PATON DAVIES
   Foreign and Other Affairs   N330

HERBERT FEIS
   The Diplomacy of the Dollar   N333

HERBERT FEIS
   The Spanish Story   N339

HERBERT FEIS
   Three International Episodes:
      Seen from E. A.   N351

DEWEY W. GRANTHAM
   The Democratic South   N299

FLETCHER GREEN
Constitutional Development in the
South Atlantic States, 1776-1860   N348

HOLMAN HAMILTON
Prologue to Conflict   N345

PENDLETON HERRING
The Politics of Democracy   N306

RUFUS JONES
The Quakers in the American Colonies   N356

GEORGE F. KENNAN
Realities of American Foreign Policy   N320

WILLIAM L. LANGER
Our Vichy Gamble   N379

DOUGLAS E. LEACH
Flintlock and Tomahawk: New England in
King Philip's War   N340

C. PETER MAGRATH
Yazoo: Law and Politics in the New Republic   N418

ALPHEUS T. MASON
The Supreme Court from Taft to Warren   N257

BURL NOGGLE
Teapot Dome   N297

DOUGLASS C. NORTH
The Economic Growth of the United States
1790-1860   N346

NORMAN POLLACK
The Populist Response to Industrial America   N295

ROBERT E. QUIRK
  An Affair of Honor: Woodrow Wilson and
    the Occupation of Veracruz   N390

ERIC ROBSON
  The American Revolution, In Its Political
    and Military Aspects: 1763-1783   N382

JAMES W. SILVER
  Confederate Morale and Church Propaganda   N422

JOHN W. SPANIER
  The Truman-MacArthur Controversy and
    The Korean War   N279

FREDERICK B. TOLLES
  Meeting House and Counting House   N211

ARTHUR BERNON TOURTELLOT
  Lexington and Concord   N194

FREDERICK JACKSON TURNER
  The United States 1830-1850   N308

HARRIS GAYLORD WARREN
  Herbert Hoover and the Great Depression   N394

ARTHUR P. WHITAKER
  The United States and the Independence
    of Latin America   N271

BRYCE WOOD
  The Making of the Good Neighbor Policy   N401

C. VANN WOODWARD
  The Battle for Leyte Gulf   N312

BENJAMIN FLETCHER WRIGHT
  Consensus and Continuity, 1776-1787   N402

IN THE NORTON LIBRARY

Aron, Raymond. *The Opium of the Intellectuals.* N106

Blair, Peter Hunter. *Roman Britain and Early England 55 B.C.–A.D. 871* N361

Bober, M. M. *Karl Marx's Interpretation of History.* N270

Brandt, Conrad. *Stalin's Failure in China.* N352

Brinton, Crane. *The Lives of Talleyrand.* N188

Brodie, Fawn. *Thaddeus Stevens.* N331

Brooke, Christopher. *From Alfred to Henry III, 871–1272* N362

Brown, Robert E. *Charles Beard and the Constitution.* N296

Burn, W. L. *The Age of Equipoise.* N319

Burnett, Edmund Cody. *The Continental Congress.* N278

Butterfield, Herbert. *The Whig Interpretation of History.* N318

Contenau, Georges. *Everyday Life in Babylon and Assyria.* N358

Cornish, Dudley Taylor. *The Sable Arm: Negro Troops in the Union Army, 1861-1865.* N334

Cortés, Hernando. *Five Letters: 1519-1526.* N180

Davies, John Paton, Jr. *Foreign and Other Affairs.* N330

De Antonio, Emile and Daniel Talbot. *Point of Order.* N10

De Roover, Raymond. *The Rise and Decline of The Medici Bank.* N350

Duckett, Eleanor. *The Wandering Saints of the Early Middle Ages* N266

Dumond, Dwight Lowell. *Antislavery* N370

Ehrenberg, Victor. *The Greek State.* N250

Erikson, Erik H. *Young Man Luther.* N170

Eyck, Erich. *Bismarck and the German Empire.* N235

Feis, Herbert. *The Diplomacy of the Dollar.* N333

Feis, Herbert. *Europe: The World's Banker 1870-1914.* N327

Feis, Herbert. *Three International Episodes: Seen from E. A.* N351

Feis, Herbert. *The Spanish Story.* N339

Ferrero, Guglielmo. *The Life of Caesar.* N111

Ferrero, Guglielmo. *The Reconstruction of Europe.* N208

Ford, Franklin L. *Strasbourg in Transition, 1648–1789* N321

Forsdyke, John. *Greece before Homer.* N240

Freeman, Kathleen. *Greek City-States.* N193

Freeman, Kathleen. *The Murder of Herodes.* N201

Freud, Sigmund, *Leonardo da Vinci and a Memory of His Childhood.* N149

Gordon, Cyrus H. *The Ancient Near East.* N275

Gordon, Cyrus H. *The Common Background of Greek and Hebrew Civilizations.* N293

Gorer, Geoffrey. *The American People.* N262

Gosse, Edmund. *Father and Son.* N195

Grantham, Dewey W. *The Democratic South.* N299

Graves, Robert and Alan Hodge. *The Long Week-end: A Social History of Great Britain, 1918-1939.* N217

Green, Fletcher. *Constitutional Development in the South Atlantic States, 1776-1860.* N348

Halperin, S. William. *Germany Tried Democracy.* N280

Hamilton, Edith. *The Echo of Greece.* N231

Hamilton, Edith. *The Greek Way.* N230

Hamilton, Edith. *The Roman Way.* N232

Hamilton, Holman. *Prologue to Conflict.* N345

Hansen, Alvin H. *The Postwar American Economy: Performance and Problems.* N236

Harrod, Roy. *The Dollar.* N191

Haskins, Charles Homer. *The Normans in European History.* N342

Herring, Pendleton. *The Politics of Democracy.* N306

Hill, Christopher. *The Century of Revolution 1603-1714.* N365

Hobsbawm, E. J. *Primitive Rebels.* N328

Holmes, George. *The Later Middle Ages 1272-1485* N363

Huntington, Ellsworth. *The Human Habitat.* N222

Jones, Rufus *The Quakers in the American Colonies* N356

Kendall, Paul Murray (editor). *Richard III: The Great Debate.* N310

Kennan, George. *Realities of American Foreign Policy.* N320

Keynes, John Maynard. *Essays in Biography.* N189

Keynes, John Maynard. *Essays in Persuasion.* N190

Langer, William L. *Our Vichy Gamble* N379

Leach, Douglass E. *Flintlock and Tomahawk: New England in King Philip's War.* N340

Maitland, Frederic William. *Domesday Book and Beyond.* N338

Mason, Alpheus Thomas. *The Supreme Court from Taft to Warren.* N257

Mason, Alpheus Thomas and William M. Beaney. *The Supreme Court in a Free Society.* N352

Mattingly, Harold. *The Man in the Roman Street.* N337

Morgenthau, Hans J. (editor). *The Crossroad Papers.* N284

Neale, J. E. *Elizabeth I and Her Parliaments,* 2 vols. N359a & N359b

Nilsson, Martin P. *A History of Greek Religion.* N287

Nilsson, Martin P. *The Mycenaean Origin of Greek Mythology.* N234

Noggle, Burl. *Teapot Dome: Oil and Politics in the 1920's.* N297

North, Douglass C. *The Economic Growth of the United States 1790-1860.* N346

Ortega y Gasset, José. *Concord and Liberty.* N124

Ortega y Gasset, José. *History as a System.* N122

Ortega y Gasset, José. *Man and Crisis.* N121

Ortega y Gasset, José. *Man and People.* N123

Ortega y Gasset, José. *Meditations on Quixote.* N125

Ortega y Gasset, José. *Mission of the University.* N127

Ortega y Gasset, José. *What Is Philosophy?* N126

Pelling, Henry. *Modern Britain 1885–1955* N368

Pendlebury, J. D. S. *The Archaeology of Crete.* N276

Pidal, Ramón Menéndez. *The Spaniards in Their History.* N353

Pollack, Norman. *The Populist Response to Industrial America.* N295

Pomper, Gerald. *Nominating the President.* N341

Robson, Eric. *The American Revolution, 1763-1783.* N382

Rostow, W. W. *The Process of Economic Growth.* N176

Roth, Cecil *The Dead Sea Scrolls: A New Historical Approach.* N303

Roth, Cecil. *The Spanish Inquisition.* N255

Rowse, A. L. *Appeasement.* N139

Russell, Bertrand. *Freedom versus Organization: 1814–1914.* N136

Salvemini, Gaetano. *The French Revolution: 1788-1792.* N179

Sinai, I. Robert. *The Challenge of Modernisation.* N323

Spanier, John W. *The Truman-MacArthur Controversy and the Korean War.* N279

Starr, Chester. *Civilization and the Caesars.* N322

Stendahl. *The Private Diaries of Stendahl.* N171

Strachey, Lytton. *Portraits in Miniature.* N181

Sykes, Norman. *The Crisis of the Reformation* N380

Taylor, F. Sherwood. *A Short History of Science & Scientific Thought.* N140

Tolles, Frederick B. *Meeting House and Counting House.* N211

Tourtellot, Arthur Bernon. *Lexington and Concord.* N194

Turner, Frederick Jackson. *The United States 1830-1850.* N308

Veblen, Thorstein. *The Instinct of Workmanship.* N265

Ward, Barbara. *India and the West.* N246

Ward, Barbara. *The Interplay of East and West.* N162

Webster, T. B. L. *From Mycenae to Homer.* N254

Whitaker, Arthur P. *The United States and the Independence of Latin America.* N271

Whyte, A. J. *The Evolution of Modern Italy.* N298

Wilcken, Ulrich. *Alexander the Great* N381

Wolfers, Arnold. *Britain and France between Two Wars.* N343

Woodward, C. Vann. *The Battle for Leyte Gulf.* N312

Woolley, C. Leonard. *The Sumerians.* N292

Woolley, C. Leonard. *Ur of the Chaldees.* N301